THE ANNEX

THE ANNEX

The Story of a Toronto Neighbourhood

JACK BATTEN

A BOSTON MILLS PRESS BOOK

© Jack Batten, 2004

First printing 2004

Library and Archives Canada Cataloguing in Publication

Batten, Jack, 1932-
The Annex : the story of a Toronto neighbourhood / Jack Batten.
Includes bibliographical references and index.

ISBN 1-55046-401-9

1. The Annex (Toronto, Ont.) – History. 2. The Annex (Toronto,
Ont.) – Biography. 3. Toronto (Ont.) – History.
4. Toronto (Ont.) – Biography. I. Title.

FC3097.52.B38 2004   971.3'541   C2004-902871-5

Publisher Cataloging-in-Publication Data   **(U.S.)**

Batten, Jack, 1932-
The Annex : the story of a Toronto neighbourhood / Jack Batten.
[160] p. : photos. ; cm.
Includes bibliographical references and index.

Summary: An illustrated history of the Annex neighborhood of Toronto: its
people, buildings, institutions, events.
ISBN 1-55046-401-9

1. Toronto (Ont.) – History – Pictorial works. 2. Neighborhood – Ontario
– Toronto. I. The Annex : the story of a Toronto neighborhood / Jack
Batten. II. Title.

971.3541   dc22   F1059.5.T686A5.B38 2004

Published in 2004 by BOSTON MILLS PRESS
132 Main Street,
Erin, Ontario N0B 1T0
Tel 519-833-2407
Fax 519-833-2195
books@bostonmillspress.com
www.bostonmillspress.com

With photographs by Sheree-Lee Olson
Editor: Kathleen Fraser
Design: PageWave Graphics Inc.

IN CANADA:
Distributed by Firefly Books Ltd.
66 Leek Crescent
Richmond Hill, Ontario L4B 1H1

IN THE UNITED STATES:
Distributed by Firefly Books (U.S.) Inc.
P.O. Box 1338, Ellicott Station
Buffalo, New York 14205

The publisher acknowledges the financial support of the Government of Canada through
the Book Publishing Industry Development Program (BPIDP) for its publishing efforts.

Photo page 2: Taddle Creek Park at Bedford Road and Lowther Avenue.
Photo page 6: The Annex Dog Walker goes on a stroll with eight customers.

Printed in Canada

For Nicky, Dashiel and Madeleine

CONTENTS

Where and What Is the Annex?

AS FAR AS ANYONE can determine, "anyone" being historians, real estate salespersons and Annex residents, the first use of the word "Annex" was by an astute land developer named Simeon Janes. Janes came up with the name in 1886 when he laid out two planned subdivisions on property he owned that was bounded roughly by Bedford Road and Spadina Road on the east and west, Dupont and Bloor Streets on the north and south. The lands were not at the time part of the City of Toronto, and when Janes applied to City Council to have his new subdivisions taken in by the city, thereby becoming eligible for such services as water, sewers and paved roads, Janes or his lawyers or his public relations people referred to the subdivisions as together comprising "The Toronto Annex."

Three years earlier, in 1883, the city had annexed the Village of Yorkville, which extended on the west almost to Bedford Road. Now, in 1887, after pondering Janes' application for many months, City Council agreed to include within Toronto's broadened borders the Janes property plus an additional two blocks not owned by Janes on the west to Kendal Avenue. A year later, in 1888, yet a further annexation brought into Toronto the land stretching from Kendal to Bathurst Street and beyond all the way to Lansdowne Avenue.

The inspiration for Janes' uninspired name, the Annex, seems to have come from the mundane, though essential, act of annexation by the city. Annexation, hence "the Annex."

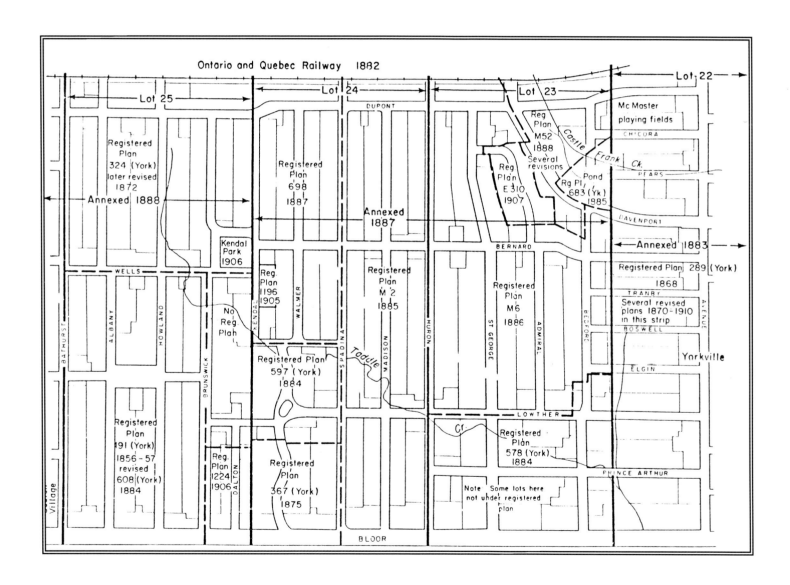

Lacking in imagination as the name was, it stuck, especially after Janes repeated it and a variation thereof, "Toronto Annexed," in advertisements for the sale of lots in the new sub-divisions. As a geographical designation, the Annex kept spreading to include blocks that had previously been known under other names. The part of the former Yorkville that lay west of Avenue Road became Annex territory, and so did both the small plot between Howland and Albany Avenues south of Wells Street, which had borne the name of St. Alban's Park for a few previous years, and a section of the much larger tract in the same neighbourhood which had gone under the name of Seaton Village. In a final addition, the Annex crept north of Dupont Street by a half block to the CPR railroad tracks that originally ran across the city's northern outskirts and made a natural Annex border.

By the time the expansions were complete, the Annex was recognized more or less officially as the part of Toronto bounded by Bloor on the south, Bathurst on the west, the CPR on the north and Avenue Road on the east. In later years, realtors who had notions of cashing in on the Annex's cachet as a chic district in which to own an address insisted on applying the Annex label to homes they were trying to sell on Robert and Major and other streets south of Bloor, to condos north of the railroad tracks, and to semi-detacheds on the wrong side of Avenue Road. But true Annex people knew better.

Students of the University of Toronto Schools in the library, 1915.

CHAPTER ONE

Our Annex Home

ON THE DAY WE took possession of our house in the Annex, August 3, 1967, the kitchen ceiling fell in.

The house was in the Annex's far western reaches, on Albany Avenue, a north-south street one block east of Bathurst. Our number, 199, placed us near the top of Albany in the long block between Wells and Dupont. The house was semi-detached, meaning that, to the occasional embarrassment of those of us who raised our voices, the none-too-thick north wall of 199 was also the south wall of 201. The lot our house stood on was narrow, just nineteen feet across, but the property ran a generous and surprising 173.5 feet to the back fence. Like most of the other houses on the block, ours had three storeys, a front porch, and no garage or other spot to park a car except at the curb. It was a brick house, and its plain but promising appearance announced that a business-minded contractor, not a fanciful architect, had designed the place.

The fallen-in ceiling was a disturbing welcome but not the catastrophe it might have been. That was because we had immediate plans to renovate. We arrived on Albany as "whitepainters," which was a term coined by the journalist Harry Bruce in an article he wrote for the April 18, 1964, issue of *Maclean's* magazine. "'Whitepainters' is my word for people who buy a mouldy downtown house and then spend several thousand dollars to clean out the cockroaches, replace the plumbing and generally exploit the building's sweet possibilities." We converted the four poky little rooms on the first floor into one open space of living room, kitchen and dining room plus a cute acorn-shaped fireplace,

April 20, 1968: From the porch at 199 Albany, the author, Jack Batten, watches as the Reverend Don Gillies (in the Volks van) arrives to marry him and Marjorie Harris. Also looking on are Batten and Harris children, Brad and Jennifer. On the sidewalk is a local boy, Carlos, who, now in his forties, still lives on Albany.

August 22, 2001: Same view from the porch thirty-three years later. Marjorie Harris works in the garden she has created while granddaughter Madeleine keeps a close eye on things through her magnifying glass.

and on the third floor, we knocked down walls to make a large master bedroom. We had ideas for the second floor, but by then, our allotted several thousand dollars had been spent.

We were the first whitepainters on the block. That made us stand out, just as a number of other characteristics tended to differentiate us from the neighbours. Density of population in our house was one. "Only your family going to live there?" an amazed Albany man said to my wife, Marjorie Harris. "It used to be four families." Most houses on the street were home to two and three generations of relatives and to boarders and roomers who came and went. Since both Marjorie and I were writers and of English ancestry, there was also the matter of our white-collar Anglo-Saxonism. It made us distinctive on a street that embraced blue-collar multiculturalism.

Ted and Ruth, a Polish-Canadian couple, lived across the street. Ted, who had a lovely smile, was an assembler at de Havilland Aircraft, and Ruth worked at Simpson's, making the crustless miniature sandwiches that the ladies ate with their tea in the Arcadian Court. A handsome-faced banty little man named John had just moved in down the street, fresh from Portugal's Madeira Islands with his wife and four young kids, sharing the house with his brother's family. John found work in roofing. Other Portuguese immigrants lived further up the block, along with residents born in Italy and, like Ted and Ruth, in Poland. But of all the many nationalities on the street, Hungarian dominated by numbers. Among the many such households, two were on either side of us, Lazlo, a man who did heavy lifting for the city, at 201, and Steve, on workmen's compensation with a permanently bad back, at 197.

Steve, in his late forties, rotund, with a stentorian voice, was the block's troubled, prickly presence. In his Hungarian hometown, Steve had suffered the death of a child and had emigrated alone to Canada where he worked as a bricklayer for eleven years until he saved enough money to bring his wife to the country — there were no other children — and to buy the house on Albany. Steve's wife, who hadn't a block identity beyond "Steve's wife," spoke no English, and his own facility with the language remained minimal. Having

Albany Avenue is in the far western reaches of the Annex, running north from Bloor Street, one block east of Bathurst.

LEFT: *The house at 199 Albany Avenue, built in 1903 by a contractor named Allaziah Norman, has a plain but promising look that is common to the street.*

The lot that 199 Albany sits on is shaped like a bowling alley, narrow (19 feet) and long (173.5 feet).

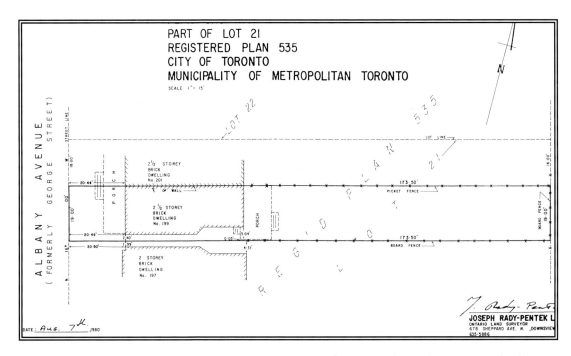

PART OF LOT 21
REGISTERED PLAN 535
CITY OF TORONTO
MUNICIPALITY OF METROPOLITAN TORONTO
SCALE 1" : 15'

JOSEPH RADY-PENTEK L
ONTARIO LAND SURVEYOR
678 SHEPPARD AVE. W. ,DOWNSVIEW
635-5886

lost much in his past, Steve guarded his present turf with zealotry that approached paranoia. He fired his BB gun at local cats who crossed his yard, confiscated children's toys that landed on his lawn, hacked off the clematis growing over a mutual fence, and provoked his neighbour on the south into a lawsuit. For two and a half decades, people on the block were united in conversations about the Steve Problem.

Edward Coath Jr. at 211 was a curiosity for more instructive reasons. He was a tall, laconic pipe-smoker, nearing retirement from his job as a foreman at Rogers Majestic. Edward Coath had lived his entire life at 211 Albany, the house that his father, Edward Sr., had helped to build in 1903. The elder Coath had been a plasterer who conducted his trade out of the house. He covered the ceilings of the first-floor rooms with samples of his work, ornate concoctions worthy of a ducal palace. Customers called on Coath the plasterer, studied the ceilings, and chose a design for their own homes. The Coath house, at the time we arrived on Albany in 1967, represented the block's best connection to its earliest history.

BADAJOZ IS A SMALL Spanish city close to the border with Portugal, its skyline identified by the ruins of a Moorish castle. On March 10, 1811, during the Peninsular Wars, Napoleon's French seized Badajoz, aided by a large bribe they slipped to the Spanish commander. The Duke of Wellington retook the city a year later in a ferocious battle that cost the British 5,000 soldiers.

One of the lucky survivors among the Brits was a colonel named Joseph Wells, thirty-nine years old and the son of a well-to-do London silk merchant. After Badajoz, Wells returned to London, married Harriett King, and sailed with her for Canada where he had accepted a post as inspector of Upper Canada's militia in the Town of York. Alas for Wells, he arrived to find that, while he was at sea, the inspector's job had been dispensed with. He settled in York anyway and was hailed by the locals as the hero of Badajoz.

In 1821, Wells bought Lot 25 in the Second Concession from the Bay, in the Home District of York, from a widow named McGill. Lot 25 was 200 acres in size; it covered much of what later became the west Annex since, in today's terms, the land was bounded by Bloor Street on the south, Bathurst on the west, St. Clair to the north, and a line extending Brunswick Avenue on the east. Mrs. McGill's late husband, John, a member of the Queen's Rangers, had been the recipient of Lot 25 as a land grant from the crown to members of the military. The grant was not of prime property for urban living, lying two inconvenient miles beyond York's settled neighbourhoods, but Lot 25 and the adjacent lots were gathering favour among the local moneyed class as a location for summer homes. The main attraction derived from the high escarpment that ran across the centre of the lots; the escarpment had been created centuries earlier when a huge glacial lake that covered the area receded after millions of year to the level of about the present Lake Ontario. John McGill (not one of the moneyed class but thinking like one) built the first house on the escarpment, situated pleasingly above the present Davenport Road. "Davenport" happened to be the name that McGill gave to the house and property in honour of a York Garrison major of that name whom McGill admired.

In 1821, Colonel Joseph Wells took up ownership of 200 acres of York land that included the property that eventually became the most westerly section of the Annex, embracing, among other streets, Albany Avenue.

Colonel Wells built his home on the hill overlooking Davenport Road near Bathurst. The house, itself called Davenport, was roomy enough to accommodate the ten Wells children.

The name of the property remained after Joseph Wells purchased it, but almost everything else changed. Wells tore down McGill's house and built a rambling three-storey home of his own, roomy enough to accommodate his eventual crowd of eight sons and two daughters. He also stepped up the already existing market gardening on the land, growing orchards of fruit and fields of vegetables. Wells kept himself busy in York politics and society, though not always to good purpose. He was a particular flop as treasurer of the new school for boys, Upper Canada College, which his own sons attended. The colonel's casual way with accounts and receipts generated a scandal among other UCC parents, who insisted that he stick to his role of gentleman farmer.

Wells died in 1853, and the Davenport property, divided into three north-south strips, passed to three of the Wells sons. Arthur got the most westerly strip, the one immediately abutting Bathurst Street. Over the following decades, the Wells brothers cooperated with businessmen and politicians in organizing the development of the Wells lands into planned subdivisions. This was not a speedy process, and it wasn't until the 1880s that the first modest house construction took place on the top block of Albany Avenue (which was first named George Street in memory of Arthur Wells' eldest brother, who died in 1854, before its change to Albany as tribute to Queen Victoria's youngest son, the Duke of Albany). The small burst of 1880s building on upper Albany produced just eleven houses in three scattered groupings on the west side of the street. The houses were first occupied for the most part by men working on the Ontario and Quebec Railroad (later bought by the CPR), which passed through the neighbourhood just north of Dupont.

The eccentric arrangement of these first Albany houses, particularly their absence from the street's east side, was explained in part by Taddle Creek's awkward presence. Taddle Creek was the name given to a stream that meandered from its headwaters on the hill west of the Davenport homestead through the Annex and the University of Toronto grounds, then skirted the downtown all the way to the bay at the foot of Parliament Street. For decades, clear and sparkling, Taddle Creek babbled along its route, producing the occasional graceful pond. The prettiest of these formed on the present site of the university's Wycliffe College and Hart House, but there were smaller ponds in the west Annex, including one on the east side of Albany at the spot where the Coath house was later built. It was this pond, plus the surrounding marshy ground, that helped to keep house construction on Albany to a minimum.

By the early 1880s, pollution had spoiled Taddle Creek's charm. Residents of Yorkville to the east turned the stream into a dumping spot for their waste, and pet owners developed the nasty custom of consigning unwanted cats and dogs to the Taddle. The water began to give off a repulsive stench, and the university put pressure on the city to eliminate the open sewer that the once lovely stream had become. In May 1884, a contractor named A.J. Brown won the tender to enclose Taddle Creek in underground pipes at a cost of $15,495.

With the stream no longer an obstacle, Albany was ripe for development, but poor Arthur Wells, who must have inherited his father's feckless business gene, was not the man who cashed in on the street's new possibilities. Arthur's prospects of profiting from

his holdings weren't aided by the economic downturn of the 1890s when Toronto's real estate market flattened and the city's home-building went into a long stall. In October 1894, Arthur gave a mortgage for $8,500 on most of his land to the Toronto General Trust Corporation. When he defaulted on his payments, Toronto General seized the property and disposed of it under a Notice of Sale in April 1901. Real estate developers and building contractors swooped in to buy parcels of Albany land, and the sound of hammers and saws at last rang over the former market gardens. By the end of 1902, new brick houses lined most of the block.

Numbers 199 and 201 Albany were among the final houses to be built. A contractor with the biblical-sounding name of Allaziah Norman, who lived around the corner on Howland Avenue, completed the two in the late autumn of 1903, and after a few years as a rental property, 199 was purchased by Robert and Euphemia Hammill. Robert was a partner at the Hammill & Hammill Real Estate Company downtown on Victoria Street, and he, Euphemia and their children lived in the house for the next half century.

Robert's occupation made him a rare white-collar resident on the Albany block. Apart from the occasional clergyman and insurance agent, most of the Hammill neighbours were in manual trades. Plumber, carpenter, watchman, lithographer, bookbinder, brass polisher — these were the jobs at which Albany men earned their incomes in the years through post-World War II. They were blue collar, and they were overwhelmingly of British background.

One part of this dual identity began to change in the early 1950s. The people who became residents of Albany's upper block for the next two decades continued to be those employed in manual work, but their ancestry was no longer predominantly Anglo-Saxon. The WASPs of Albany had joined others from Toronto's central core in the flight to the new suburbs, to Don Mills, Scarborough and Etobicoke. They were attracted by large houses and wide lots, by garages and the privacy of relatively vast distances from the neighbours next door. What they left behind on Albany was inexpensive housing, which became a point of destination for immigrants freshly arrived in unprecedented numbers from continental Europe. The upper block of Albany had taken a sudden turn to multiculturalism.

Through most of the nineteenth century, the land that was to become Albany Avenue and the rest of the west Annex looked much like the farming properties shown in the this 1880s painting of north St. George Street.

The succeeding owners of 199 Albany after Robert Hammill's estate sold it in 1950 had names that were typical of the block: Goldmacher, Eisener, Podlisker, Hamajda and Honik. Many of them were absentee owners, renting the house by the floor or by the room to tenants who were in most cases, like themselves, new to Toronto. The house's rental possibilities reached the bursting point in the three years before we bought it, when four family groups in numbers we could never determine called 199 home. They lived one family or one person per floor, including the basement, and shared one conventional kitchen, one mini-kitchen, two bathrooms, and one bathtub. Then we arrived as owners, bringing our whitepainter notions, and the house underwent a metamorphosis. So, beginning in the mid-1970s, did the whole Albany block.

The old guard: Ted, shown here, and his wife, Ruth, moved into 174 Albany in 1957. Ted was born in Poland and worked as an assembler at de Havilland Aircraft. (The dog's name is Dallas.)

The new wave: Diana and her husband, Bruce, a lawyer, arrived on Albany in 1993 as the new owners of number 197. Diana was born in Ghana, took an engineering degree at Queen's University, works in management, and together with Bruce, raises their two children.

ON A WEEKDAY AFTERNOON in May 1993, two airport limousines pulled up at 197 Albany, the house of our prickly neighbour, Steve. The limo drivers staggered back and forth from the house's front hall to the cars shouldering a succession of trunks and suitcases, bound in rope and bearing Steve's worldly goods. A few months earlier, Steve's wife had died, and now he was moving on — out of the house, off the block, away from Canada. Steve was returning to his Hungarian birthplace. Some of us came from our houses and shook Steve's hand, aware that we had never managed a neighbourly connection with him nor even negotiated a lasting truce. Steve climbed into the front seat of the first limo, the other seats of both cars stacked with luggage, and the small convoy carried Steve away from the home he had uncomfortably inhabited for a quarter of a century.

Within a month, Bruce and Diana moved into 197. Bruce was from Montreal, a lawyer in corporate work. Diana grew up in Ghana, where many of her family still lived; she had an engineering degree from Queen's University but now planned to stay at home and start a family. Bruce and Diana renovated much of the house and replaced the kitchen, which hadn't been touched since April 28, 1950. They could be specific about the date because they found secreted in one wall a page of the *Toronto Star* of that day together with a pen-cilled note written in an artless hand. "I came to Canada from England in 1947. I have remodelled this kitchen. I know one day it will be pulled down, it will be for you to say how long this is." The note identified its author as Ernest Frederick Bower. Mr. Bower had owned and lived in the house for seven years and had worked in Toronto's plastering trade.

Albany Avenue lampposts carry news of everything from nudist parks to garage sales by "coolio chicks."

Steve's departure and Bruce and Diana's arrival marked one more step in a process that had been underway for more than fifteen years. Almost all of the blue-collar immigrants who had settled the block in the 1950s and 1960s were giving way to younger couples with university educations and whitepainter intentions. Steve was unique in abandoning Canada; his fellow Hungarian-Canadians on the street, along with the neighbours of Portuguese, Italian and other continental European ancestry, imitated the original Anglo-Saxon residents in the flight to Toronto's suburbs. In all other ways, the turnover at 197 Albany fit the pattern that we had been watching in houses up and down the block over the preceding decade and a half: baby boomer and post-boomer couples snapping up the properties, keen to live downtown in the Annex, prepared to renovate and to raise kids.

Bruce and Diana were also typical in coming from somewhere other than Toronto and, in Diana's case, somewhere other than Canada. Across the street, a woman from Morocco moved in. In another house, the husband was from Switzerland, the wife from Montreal. There was an Israeli husband and a Mexican wife, a man from the Caribbean married to a woman from Scotland, an English couple, a man in one house who grew up on Long Island, and a man in another who didn't mind Toronto winters because he said it was colder in Wisconsin where he spent his childhood. The old Coath house became home to a woman who was English born and a man of English-Yugoslav background, both of whom took enormous pride in the elaborate plaster designs on their first-floor ceilings.

The block had almost as much multiplicity of origin as before, except now the residents were more affluent, more educated and more cosmopolitan, a demographical fact that was reflected in the new homeowners' occupations. A teacher in the art department at Jarvis Collegiate, a professor of English literature at York, an administrator at the University of

Toronto — we had plenty of educators in our midst. Not to mention an executive from Amnesty International and the head of the Evergreen Foundation. There was a woman who wrote TV documentaries on environmental issues, and another woman who was a Queen's Park lawyer working on legislative matters. A social worker, a leading actor in the Toronto theatre and on Canadian TV, a psychologist, a man who made his money as a school textbook publisher until he quit to become a ceramist — all of these now lived on Albany. And so did a couple who were the proprietors of a popular Bloor Street restaurant specializing in Mediterranean dishes.

Activism arrived on the street too, largely in the form of a neighbourhood group called Grassroots Albany that materialized in the early 1990s as a block environmental force. Its purpose was to protect the neighbourhood's ecology, and to that end, it produced a forty-three-page report titled "Inventory and Natural History of the Albany Neighbourhood Forest." The report told everyone on the block about the nature and health of the trees on their land. "The next step," the report concluded, "is for the community to develop a plan to manage its unique urban forest." Over the following decade, homeowners on the block chopped down dying trees and planted new trees and foliage that were native to the area.

It would be stretching the truth to say that, in its changing character, the upper block of Albany could be regarded as a microcosm for the rest of the Annex. Other Annex neighbourhoods had very different histories. Some of the more prominent of these began as the enclaves of wealthy Torontonians, then saw the mansions undergo conversion to rooming houses during hard times, eventually returning to single family status when the Annex once again became fashionable. Each small area of the Annex, even each street within each area, had its own story. Our houses on Albany weren't as large and expensive as those even one street over on Howland Avenue and were no match in architectural splendour for the array of Victorian, Queen Anne and Richardsonian-Romanesque structures further east. But in many other respects — in the high rate of renovation, in the majority of professionals in residence, in pride of neighbourhood, in a faintly snobby self-consciousness about living close to the heart of the city — Albany had emerged in our own three and a half decades at 199 as pure and representative Annex.

CHAPTER TWO

How the Annex Grew

TIMOTHY EATON WASN'T THE richest man in Toronto in the last decades of the nineteenth century, or the most famous, but he was the city's most famous rich man, and in 1889, by moving into his new mansion at 182 Lowther Avenue on the northwest corner of Spadina Road, he confirmed that the Annex, even the relative wilderness of the west Annex, was a very good address.

At the time Eaton took up the Lowther residence, he had reached his early sixties. His eponymous department store had been in business since 1869 and was fast growing into a retailing empire. Timothy was a close man with a buck, but he was earning so many bucks that by the 1880s, he was indulging himself and his family, which consisted of his wife, Margaret, his two daughters and three sons. He acquired a lavish summer home on prime Muskoka land, a 54-foot yacht, three other rural properties, and the Lowther mansion, which Mrs. Eaton crowded with French gilt furniture, pointe de Venise lace curtains, glass cases displaying ornate doodads, and Moorish touches not always in the best of taste. The house became a place of suburban refuge for Timothy and family. It was isolated from the urban racket of his previous home on Orde Avenue south of College Street, and it was surrounded by the silence of vacant lots both on Spadina and, with the major exception of Walmer Road Baptist Church to the west, on Lowther.

The historic mansion at Spadina and Lowther where Timothy Eaton made his home in 1889 is shown here shortly before its demolition in the 1960s.

Timothy found his part of the Annex so blissful that he made sure at least two of his adult children likewise lived in the neighbourhood. In 1901, he bought a new house at 60 Spadina just north of Lowther for his second daughter, Margaret Elizabeth, and her husband, Charles Burden, and the same year, he performed a similar deed for his newly married youngest son, Jack, purchasing and furnishing a house at 121 Walmer. Jack was a special case, the son whom Timothy designated as his successor to the T. Eaton Co. presidency. As a young man, Jack differed from his father, a virtual teetotaller, in his affection for booze. This so alarmed the senior Eatons that, in 1900, they despatched

The style of decor in the rooms and halls of Timothy Eaton's mansion was lavish, ornate and not always in the best of taste.

Jack to Rotherham House, a small twenty-bed hospital on Isabella Street where the patients' meals came on china dishes with silver in a fine English pattern. While taking the cure at Rotherham, Jack became entranced by a student nurse. She was Flora McCrae, the daughter of a cabinet maker in Omemee, Ontario. Jack proposed, and the two were married on May 8, 1901.

Jack and Flora — eventually Sir John and Lady Eaton — were delighted to return from their honeymoon and move into the new three-storey brick house on Walmer. It came with a full-time maid and a weekly charwoman but without an indoor parking

place for Jack's precious Winton automobile. Jack remedied the oversight by buying a 50-foot lot north of the house and building a two-car garage. As Lady Eaton later observed, it was "the first of such structures, designed especially for the purpose and placed near the house, to go up in Toronto." The garage became home in 1906 to Jack's Rolls-Royce, purchased from Charles Rolls himself. This was another first for Jack, making him the first owner of a Rolls-Royce not just in the Annex or Toronto but in all of Canada.

IN THE LATE SPRING of 1793, a century before Timothy Eaton and his offspring were spreading the wealth in and around the Annex, John Graves Simcoe paddled into Toronto harbour and liked what he saw. Simcoe, who had recently been appointed Upper Canada's governor, was a military man, and he reasoned that the tidiness of the harbour, sheltered by a peninsula (later separated into Toronto Island), offered a promising site for defence against a possible invasion by the troublesome Americans. In Simcoe's view, there was only one drawback to Toronto: the name. It had to go. Toronto, an Indian appellation, meant "place of meeting" in one interpretation and "much or many" in another. Simcoe wanted something that had a more warlike connotation and renamed the new outpost York in honour of the second son of George III. The son was Frederick Augustus, the Duke of York, and he had led a successful battle against the French Revolutionary Army at Famars in Holland on May 24 of that very year, 1793 (the Duke's record in later 1790s battles was spotty, if not downright deplorable).

Simcoe had been preceded in the choice spot he called York by centuries of Indians and decades of traders, explorers and soldiers, principally from France and Britain. The area was rich in game, fruit trees and fish, and it made a convenient departure point for a shortcut to the upper Great Lakes by way of the Humber River and beyond. In 1615, Etienne Brûlé was the first recorded white person to visit Toronto. He was a trapper, smart and intrepid but so ornery that the Huron slew Brûlé and, one historian reported, served him for dinner. Other whites stopping by Toronto never found themselves on the local menu, but apart from establishing the occasional fort and trading post, neither did any of them settle in for the long haul until Simcoe arrived.

He applied his military mind to the orderly and precise laying out of a town. Everything was in grids, even where ravines and streams intervened, and principal streets appeared at appropriate and evenly spaced intervals. To the north, Simcoe made Bloor Street the First Concession Line in York Township, the boundary dividing the Town of York from park lots on the street's north side. The Village of Yorkville shaped itself around the corner of Bloor and Yonge Street, and to the west of Yonge, at regular distances of one-eighth of a mile, lots of 200 acres extended north from Bloor to St. Clair Avenue. It was on the lower halves of the lots closest to Yonge, numbers 22 through 25, that the Annex would eventually take shape.

York's population reached 9,000 in 1834, the year that it was incorporated as a city and reverted to its pre-Simcoe name of Toronto. One of the city's leading citizens was the polymath William Warren Baldwin, teacher, lawyer, doctor, amateur architect and dabbler in political theory. Through an 1813 inheritance by his wife, the former Phoebe Willcocks, Baldwin acquired one of the 200-acre lots between Bloor and St. Clair, lot number 24. The Baldwin property lay to the immediate east of what was then the McGill lot, shortly to be purchased by Colonel Joseph Wells, the hero of Badajoz. In 1818, Baldwin designed and built a home at his land's highest point, the hill overlooking the city, and called it Spadina House. The name, adapted from *epadinong*, an Indian word for "a hill" or, less prosaically, "a sudden rise of ground," was pronounced *spa-dee-na*.

Four years later, much of the 200-acre lot next door on the east, number 23, came under Baldwin's control when its owner, the childless widow Elizabeth Russell, died and willed the land to her cousins, Phoebe Willcocks Baldwin and Maria Willcocks. In 1835, Spadina House burned down. Within the year, Baldwin designed and built a smaller version of the home. During the same period, as part of his development for housing of lands south of Bloor Street (originally Russell property), he fashioned a spectacular road leading

William Warren Baldwin, physician, lawyer, teacher and amateur architect, designed Spadina Avenue and was an early owner of the lands that his grandson, William Willcocks Baldwin, later developed as the west Annex.

The view in this 1880s photograph is north on Bedford from Lowther. Within a decade, the farmland was turned to housing developments.

from the city north to Bloor. It was 132 feet wide for much of its length, and was named Spadina Avenue, though in the instance of the street, Torontonians insisted on pronouncing it *spa-di-na*.

William Warren Baldwin died in 1844, and under the stewardship of his son Robert, known to Ontario history as "the father of Responsible Government," the Spadina lands remained largely intact. But the next generation of Baldwins, principally Robert's son, William Willcocks Baldwin, presided over both the dismantling and the development of the Baldwin estate. The development phase included the laying out in the 1870s of two significant Annex streets, Walmer Road and Spadina Road, each of which boasted special distinctions. Walmer's lower blocks emerged in the Baldwin design in snaky curves, one of the few Annex streets, along with the upper bit of Admiral Road and a couple of jogs in Dupont and one jog each in Bedford Road and Bernard Avenue, that wasn't described in straight lines. As for Spadina Road, it was a narrower extension of the glorious Spadina

Avenue, running on a slight northeast bias to the foot of the hill beneath Spadina House.

The house itself, along with eighty surrounding acres, disappeared from Baldwin hands at auction to James Austin, the founder and president of the Dominion Bank. He demolished the existing Spadina House and erected his own version of a grand residence (one that survives to this day). The Baldwins also unloaded at reduced prices the southern sections of their original estate, notably the part that lay east of Spadina Avenue and south of Davenport, to Simeon Janes, the slick developer who, in financial terms, appears to have picked the Baldwins' pocket. Janes was a lawyer, a dry goods dealer and a lover of fine art as well as a developer. He parlayed his expertise in real estate into a fortune that provided him with most of life's good things, a catalogue that climaxed at the top of the hill on Avenue Road in his massive mansion, known as Benvenuto.

Janes' plans of subdivision on the land west of the original Yorkville and east of Spadina were of straight streets with large homes on smallish lots for a well-to-do clientele. He envisioned neighbourhoods that would be genteel and strictly residential. That meant no room for commercial enterprises nor for public buildings, no alleyways to speak off (hence the later lack of garages for cars and today's horrendous Annex parking problem), but it meant generous setbacks from the street for the houses, a circumstance that made for rows of roomy front lawns. The purchasers of the Janes lots and the contractors who built the houses on the lots stuck to the Janes vision. As a result, the Annex that began to emerge in the late nineteenth century, allowing for occasional delays that the economic slowdown of the 1890s brought on, was one that the Toronto historian G. Mercer Adams characterized as "the condition of perfect community [with] implicit confidence put in the civility and good will of neighbours."

Some especially wealthy Torontonians didn't need Janes' encouragement to choose the Annex or, at any rate, the Annex's borders, as the site of their homes. Slightly ahead of Janes, in 1892, George Gooderham of the Gooderham & Worts liquor fortune completed his mansion, undoubtedly the most handsome building ever erected in the Annex, at the northeast corner of St. George and Bloor. And fifteen years before that, Albert Nordheimer of the Nordheimer piano manufacturing family had put up his expensive residence at the northwest corner of Bloor and Avenue Road. But the Janes notion of suburban living for

From St. George Street looking east between Dupont and Bernard in 1890, the skyline shows the tower of the Church of the Messiah at Dupont and Avenue Road.

the upper middle class, a concept that was echoed in the development of the Baldwin lands west of Spadina Road, caught on in a big way with Toronto's freshly thriving professional, business and manufacturing classes. Lawyers and accountants with fine downtown firms moved in; Geoffrey Clarkson of Clarkson, Gordon, for example, at 88 Walmer. So did such nouveau riche as George Hees (maker of window shades and curtains) at 174 St. George and Sigmund Samuel (manufacturer of the newfangled metallic ceilings and dealer in the ever profitable scrap metal trade) at 32 Walmer. These were the sort of Torontonians — good manners, money in the bank, inoffensive taste in architecture — who populated the Annex.

The less affluent had their Annex place too, mostly on the fringes. Albany's upper block with its tiny lots and its population of manual workers was repeated on Howland's upper block and, further east, on such other Annex margins as Tranby Avenue. But they hardly set the tone for the Annex as Janes and the other real estate moguls developed it. That was left to the residents on proud and prosperous Prince Arthur and Lowther and St. George, though, as the Annex's history unfolded, few of these trend-setting families stuck around into their third and fourth generations. Sometimes one generation of Annex living was enough.

TIMOTHY EATON DIED IN his bed in the mansion at 182 Lowther on January 31, 1907. He had been ill for several days with a high fever, his lungs filling with fluid, but in an odd display of priorities, Timothy's wife, Margaret, and son Jack had traveled to Ottawa for a performance by a group from one of Mrs. Eaton's pet projects, the Margaret Eaton School of Literature and Expression. Their absence left only Jack's wife, Flora, at Timothy's bedside when he succumbed to pneumonia.

Madison Avenue south from Dupont was raw and new and without trees in 1910, not long after the street's house construction was completed.

MADISON AVE.
TORONTO

The portly gentleman in the middle is Jack — later Sir John — Eaton, son of Timothy and his successor as president of the T. Eaton Company. The lad in the nurse's arms is Jack's son and a future Eaton president, John David Eaton.

OPPOSITE: *Jack Eaton built this fifty-room mansion called Ardwold on ten acres at the top of the hill above Davenport Road. When he moved into it in 1911 after two decades in the Annex, he sent an early signal of a shift among wealthy Torontonians out of the Annex.*

With the great merchandiser's demise, Jack succeeded to the presidency of the ever expanding Eaton empire. Not long into the job, Jack and Flora decided that their house at 121 Walmer wasn't suited to their new station and to their duties to Toronto commerce and society. They needed a more substantial residence. Accordingly in 1909, they purchased from Albert Austin, son of James Austin, ten acres at the top of the hill above Davenport Road to the east of Spadina House. The Eatons spent two years in building the palatial home they called Ardwold, Gaelic for "high green hill." Ardwold, which Jack and Flora moved into in 1911, had fifty rooms including fourteen bathrooms, an indoor swimming pool, a two-storey Great Hall with a giant pipe organ, and a small two-bed hospital, fully equipped for surgery. It was in his own mini-hospital that Jack — or Sir John, as he

became in 1915 — lay ill with pneumonia and a general infection for nine weeks in early 1922 until he died on March 30, just forty-six years old.

Jack and Flora's relocation to Ardwold from Walmer Road anticipated by a decade and a half the beginning of the shift among wealthy people out of the Annex in favour of such more exclusive neighbourhoods as Rosedale and Forest Hill. The reasons for the Annex exodus had much to do with fear and snobbery. Many of the most prosperous residents left for Eaton-like reasons: to build palatial residences, though hardly on an Ardwold scale, in urban surroundings where there was more elbow room than the densely packed Annex offered. But far more Annex first families seem to have been scared off by what they viewed as an alarming social upheaval. The male breadwinners in too many Annex homes were dying off, leaving behind widows who couldn't support the houses on their late husbands' insurance and the rest of their widows' mites. They discreetly let out rooms. Such a habit grew less discreet and more visible. Mansions became rooming houses and boarding houses, and in reaction, respectable Annex people, the descendents of the originals, moved out.

Other factors came into annoying play in the Annex's relative deterioration in the years immediately after World War II. When the University of Toronto expropriated properties on St. George south of Bloor to build Innis College and other academic centres, the fraternities whose chapters had occupied the street's ancient mansions purchased other ancient mansions north of Bloor as replacements. Frat rushing parties, hijinks on front lawns and cranked-up pop music from open windows became irritants of life on Madison, Lowther and upper St. George. Small commercial enterprises — psychologists' consulting rooms, editorial offices for magazines of modest circulation, quarters for charitable foundations — also set up on the floors of former single-family dwellings. And trade in illegal drugs hit the Annex in the 1960s. Among themselves, Howland's residents referred to their street as "Speed Alley" in recognition of the trafficking in amphetamines that went on after dark, and the lower part of Admiral Road thrived as the operating quarters for dealers in soft drugs.

The Annex lost its early dazzle, though all was not lost. Professors from the nearby university bought Annex houses. So did other middle-class people looking for a bargain

The houses on Tranby Avenue, shown here in the 1960s, were first built at the turn of the century for working-class residents.

A newspaper kiosk, a streetcar stop, and overhang of leafy trees — this was the corner of Bloor and Spadina, looking south down Spadina Avenue, in August 1944.

and willing to tolerate the fraternities and drug culture. Homeowners who weren't of the absentee variety kept the old houses in liveable condition, and the ratepayers association that had first come together in the early 1920s reenergized itself to keep the developers and other barbarians at bay. The Annex was in readiness for the day, due to arrive in the early 1970s, when the area became trendy in a different way than Simeon James had imagined.

TIMOTHY EATON'S WIDOW, MARGARET, survived him until 1934. She divided her time principally between the family's Muskoka summer home, an elaborate place in Oakville, and the mansion at 182 Walmer. In 1929, Margaret gave the Walmer house to her divorced daughter, Josephine Burnside, who kept it for five years until she made a gift of it to the Imperial Order Daughters of the Empire. The house served as the IODE's national headquarters for the next thirty years. In 1965, the IODE made a financial killing by selling the mansion to a developer who demolished the building and put up a fifteen-storey apartment high-rise. With those two acts of destruction and construction, the last touch of the Eaton family vanished from the Annex.

The orderly parade of handsome porches on the houses of Brunswick Avenue on a winter morning in the 1960s.

CHAPTER THREE

The Annex Look

EDWARD JAMES LENNOX, the Toronto architect who lived from 1854 to 1933 and was known to his friends and associates as "E.J.," liked to have his photograph taken, preferably in front of buildings he designed. He was a public figure, a man who got out and about in the city, a joiner, a member of the Masons, the Board of Trade and the Cameron Lloyd Orange Lodge. It was good for business to belong to such organizations, but Lennox also enjoyed the stroking that his ego received from his fellow Masons and Orangemen. Lennox was a man of much self-regard. When he completed the long and taxing task of designing and overseeing the construction of his greatest work, the building now known as Old City Hall, he arranged to have his likeness carved in stone over the centre arch of the main entrance, and much further up on the building, he cut the designation, E J LENNOX ARCHITECT 1889, into the stone under the cornice around the structure's four sides. When he built his own luxurious house in 1913 on the hill at Walmer Road above Davenport, he called it Lenwil in salute to himself in the first syllable and to his wife, whose maiden name was Wilson, in the second syllable. He was careful to position his own bedroom at the mansion's northeast corner on the second floor. This meant that each morning when he arose, his first view was across Walmer to Casa Loma, Sir Henry Pellatt's castle, which was Lennox's most ostentatious work and became probably the best-known Toronto landmark among tourists to the city.

Lennox decided on his future profession early. He would design buildings, an ambition that, coming at age fourteen, disconcerted his father, who had other ideas for young E.J.

The first Annex house that Lennox designed was in 1883 at 280 Bloor West for a wholesale clothier named William Lailey. The house has since been demolished to make way for a hotel.

Designed by E.J. Lennox in 1886, the house at 37 Madison Avenue became known as "the Annex house" for its influential combination of Richardsonian Romanesque in the lower half and Queen Anne in the upper storey.

The senior Lennox was an immigrant to Toronto from County Antrim in Ireland. He made his money in wholesale produce, real estate and the ownership of a downtown hotel near St. Lawrence Hall, and he had a similar business career in mind for his son. But E.J. insisted on studying architectural drawing at the Mechanics' Institute. He graduated at the top of a class of sixty students, an admirable feat since he was, at seventeen, by far the youngest of the group. Lennox's father, at last persuaded to E.J.'s life plan, pulled a few strings to get him an apprenticeship with a leading Toronto architect, William Irving. Five intellectually profitable years later, Lennox entered into partnership with another established architect, William Frederick McCaw. McCaw & Lennox were responsible for the designs of Bond Street Congregational Church at Bond and Dundas Streets, the Hotel Hanlan on Toronto Island and the Erskine Presbyterian Church on Elm Street. Such showy buildings, alas all demolished in later years, were the makings of E.J.'s reputation. In 1881, he opened his own office, putting himself on a path that brought him in 1886 to the watershed event of his career: a victory in the competition to design Toronto's new City Hall.

Like many other North American architects, including a significant group in Toronto, Lennox felt the influence of Henry Hobson Richardson. Richardson was a Boston-based architect who studied at the Ecole des Beaux Arts in Paris and brought the Romanesque Revival style of architecture to North America. Richardson lived a short life, dying in 1886 at age forty-eight, and he designed relatively few buildings, but they were so distinctive in the style that came to be known as Richardsonian Romanesque that dozens of architects revered his innovations and devised their own improvisations on the Richardson oeuvre. His buildings had a grand and chunky form, squared stone, plenty of high arches, roofs that ran likewise to lofty peaks, windows set deep, and lots of surprisingly delicate ornamentation. A Richardson building gave the impression that it was put together for a long lasting existence.

Lennox was particularly attracted to Richardson's 1884 Allegheny County Courthouse

Edward James Lennox, architect, left his distinctive mark on Toronto, designing, among other celebrated buildings, Old City Hall and three Annex houses.

and Jail in Pittsburgh. At the time he was preparing his own Toronto City Hall design, he reported to the local building committee that "Pittsburgh is the only city that has a building that is somewhat similar in its appointments to what your building will be." Lennox's City Hall was hardly a copy of Richardson's Allegheny Courthouse, but it exuded the same strength and vigour. It relied similarly on a largeness of scale in all things, on rough stone and impressive roofs. But, as the astute Toronto architecture writer, Patricia McHugh, points out, "Old City Hall is pictorial and ornamental in ways not found in Richardson's more intellectual, abstract granite composition." Lennox's building, which took almost fifteen years in planning, construction and fine tuning, emerged as distinctively one of a kind, exciting and confident to the point of exuberance.

The house at 234 St. George, designed by E.J. Lennox in 1902, now serves as the front for a discreet low-rise apartment complex.

In the early stages of Lennox's City Hall period, the Richardsonian Romanesque effect was also at work when he turned his mind in 1886 to a commission for a house at 37 Madison Avenue. It was a house that, probably not to the surprise of the self-assured Lennox, became recognized as an aesthetic triumph. The Madison design, incorporating Richardsonian Romanesque elements, solved so many problems in creating the ideal suburban house for the 1880s Toronto business class that it grew to be much imitated and exerted a large and immediate impact on the overall look of the rising new Annex.

In all, Lennox designed three Annex houses. The first, in 1883 and therefore predating 37 Madison, was at 280 Bloor West for a dealer in wholesale clothing named William Lailey; it emerged as a not altogether successful riff on the Queen Anne style. The third, which was post-37 Madison by a decade and a half, went up at 234 St. George Street for a client named Robert Watson who made his bundle in candy manufacturing.

*This 1894 double house
at 69 and 71 Madison
Avenue was typical of
Annex houses built in the
1890s: terracotta brick,
lots of decorative touches,
a look of solidity.*

Watson was a picky fellow and requested many designs from Lennox before he begrudged his approval. The dithering seems to have been reflected in the ultimate design, which gave the house a fancypants appearance of many disparate styles and elements.

The house at 37 Madison was a felicitous combination of just two styles, one downstairs and the other upstairs, Richardsonian Romanesque in the lower half and the more light and inventive Queen Anne in the upper half. Lennox's client was pleased and flat-

Hamilton Townsend was the architect who gave this 1901 house at 109 Walmer a snug look with its extensive use of shingles on the upper half.

tered by the solution. The lucky man's name was Lewis Lukes, and he had more than a nodding acquaintance with Lennox. Lukes was a contractor around town whose reputation took a boost when he handled part of the City Hall job for his pal E.J. The design of the Madison house, which was constructed in 1888 and 1889 (though apparently not occupied by Lukes until at least late 1890), offered a clever series of contrasts. It reflected such large and upright virtues as solidity and stability but seemed perfectly at ease on a relatively small plot of land. It looked as imperishable as the City Hall that was going up downtown, and at the

same time, it gave off a domestically fashionable air. The contractors who were building new houses in the nearby Annex blocks, mostly as speculative ventures, took note of Lennox's notions in design, of his use of stone and brick, and seized on them as models. On neighbouring parts of Madison, on Huron, St. George and other principal streets, variations on 37 Madison began to appear in substantial numbers, meaning that it was not for nothing that the Lukes residence acquired the definitive name of "the Annex house."

OPPOSITE: This 1930 photo shows the 1891 house at 62 Bernard in all its Queen Anne glory.

An early Annex apartment building, dating from 1906 at 93 to 99 Madison Avenue, blended seamlessly into the neighbourhood with its red brick and its projecting windows.

Most Annex houses owed their design to the contractors who built them, but many of Lennox's contemporaries in Toronto architecture had their bright Annex moments. Frederick Herbert was a designer of surprises. At 88 Madison, he put up a house in 1899 that was dominated by its eye-catching tower; all larger Annex houses had towers but none so charming and goofy as this one. In 1901, Hamilton Townsend departed from the Annex norm with his design at 109 Walmer of a house that did wonderful things with exterior walls of shingles. And at 260 St. George, Eden Smith excelled himself with his 1905 design in the Cottage Style, of which he was regarded as the local master.

Lennox's trend-starting house at 37 Madison, which contributed most in giving the Annex the invariable look of red stone and solid substance at its well-to-do core, enjoyed a history that reflects the history of the Annex itself. Succeeding Lewis Lukes in residence during the Annex's first heyday was a notable local personage, James Grace, treasurer of the Toronto Railway. By the 1920s, nobody less than a knight, Sir James Aird of the Canadian Bank of Commerce, had settled in. After the Second World War, the house was divided into apartments, the fate of most of its neighbours, but the apartments at number 37 were roomy and smart and attracted a classy brand of tenant. Don Ketcheson was one, a leading Toronto interior designer from the 1960s to the end of the century. The live-in tenants gave way to office spaces in the 1980s. In the 1990s, MPI Productions restored the house to one-occupant unity. MPI — the letters stand for nothing — took over 37 Madison and, aware of the building's honourable history, devoted the first six months of ownership to spiffing up both interior and exterior. Today, still under MPI's aegis, the house is as

Spadina Gardens at 41-45 Spadina Road, erected in 1905, was an apartment building that offered tenants elegance in design and exceptionally roomy apartments.

Designed by Eden Smith in 1905,
the house at 260 St. George is a
formidable but comfortable example of
Smith's Cottage Style of architecture.

close to Lennox's original plan as the twenty-first century allows while activity inside is given over to a business — video post-production — that would have been beyond nineteenth-century comprehension.

In this 1902 house at 343 Brunswick, the architect allowed, uniquely, for three miniature columns on the porch.

Of Lennox's two other Annex houses, the one at 234 St. George survives as the showpiece of an intelligently integrated low-rise apartment complex while the other, the Lailey house at 280 Bloor West, has been demolished in favour of the Quality Hotel Midtown. Many of Lennox's once-admired Toronto buildings have gone the demolition route. But among those that remain intact, Lenwil, Lennox's residence, stands out, faithfully maintained by its occupants since 1948, a Ukrainian religious order named the Sister Servants of Mary Immaculate Christ the King. Tourists continue to adore Casa Loma, though critics have been much less kind to its design; "hard to live down" was how Eric Arthur disparaged this florid example of Lennox's work in *No Mean City*, Arthur's great study of Toronto architecture. Lennox shared design credit in 1902 with the Chicago architect Henry Ives Cobb for the still elegant King Edward Hotel (the elaborate main dining room was pure Lennox). And his Bank of Toronto at 205 Yonge Street (1905), home in later years to the Toronto Historical Board, reigns as the city's most splendid building in the Beaux Art mode.

Lenwil was the last building of consequence that Lennox designed before he closed his office in 1917. Retirement didn't mean he tossed aside his devotion to architecture. He continued to mentor younger members of the profession, and in 1931, when the Ontario legislature passed a bill that at last granted official accreditation to the province's architects, Lennox was prompt in signing up even though he was seventy-seven and no longer a practising architect. He passed his days at Lenwil, strolling the two and a half acres of property, a pet parrot perched on his shoulder, and taking regular drives around town in his seven-passenger Pierce Arrow sedan. He died on April 15, 1933, and was buried from St. Paul's Anglican Church on Bloor Street East. The church, robust and Gothic-inspired, happened to be a building that Lennox designed in 1909. He charged no fee for the job, a sign of both his piety and of the level of wealthy success he had reached in the profession he chose at a very young age.

The double house at 99-101 Howland Avenue is known as the candle-snuffer house for its eccentric roof decor.

OPPOSITE: *This row of pleasantly erratic houses on Lowther Avenue, including one in the foreground with a carriageway, dates from the 1870s when the street was part of Yorkville village.*

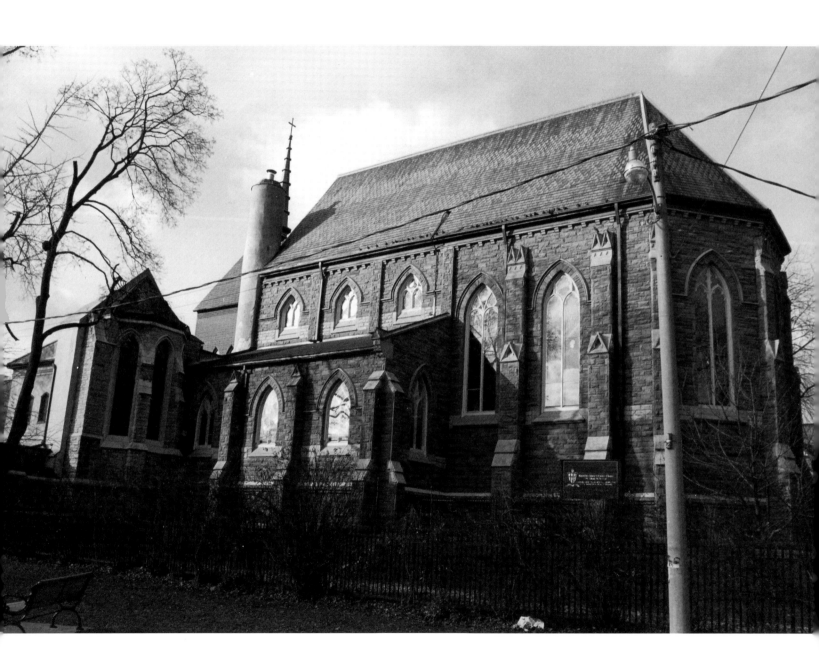

CHAPTER FOUR

An Annex Cathedral

and Other Institutions of the Spirit and Mind

ARTHUR SWEATMAN ASCENDED TO the Anglican Church's top job in the Diocese of Toronto in 1879. He rejoiced in the designation of Archbishop Metropolitan of the Ecclesiastical Province of Ontario and Primate of All Canada, and as such, he adopted the personal priority of overseeing the creation at last of an Anglican cathedral in Toronto. A cathedral was not merely a church of a parish but of the entire diocese, something that for complex reasons of church politics, the Toronto Diocese still conspicuously lacked.

Archbishop Sweatman's progress was less than swift. In 1881, the Anglican Synod passed a resolution adopting the cathedral project. Two years later, the cathedral-to-be had a name, St. Alban the Martyr. St. Alban, regarded as the Proto-Martyr of the Anglican Church, was an officer of the Roman Army in England who embraced Christianity. This was an act of courage and folly that earned him a beheading by the Roman Governor in A.D. 304 at Verulamium, which much later was renamed St. Alban's in the County of

OPPOSITE: Designed in 1885, St. Alban the Martyr on Howland Avenue has never been completed, but until 1936, it was officially the Anglican cathedral of the Diocese of Toronto.

Hertfordshire. But the matter of a location in Toronto for the Cathedral of St. Alban the Martyr kicked around for another couple of frustrating years. Two existing churches, Holy Trinity and St. George's, were considered for upgrading to cathedral status under the new name, but Sweatman turned them down on the grounds that the buildings were not commodious enough and lacked the surrounding property for the necessary expansion. The idea that St. James, the towering neo-Gothic edifice erected in 1875 on King Street East, might fill the role foundered over one major issue. St. James had been legally established as a parish church, and its seating accommodation was therefore in the possession of pew-holders who refused to be dispossessed. Dispossession was a move that would be necessary if St. James were to become the cathedral, since no one was entitled to exercise exclusive right to a pew or a seat in a cathedral except in special circumstances. St. James parishioners, proprietorial about their pews and cranky at the notion of surrendering them, had not the slightest intention of making way for a cathedral, especially one that might be given a name other than St. James.

In 1885, in mild desperation for a location to build a cathedral from scratch, Sweatman turned to a corner of the Annex. The piece of land in question, a plot bounded by Wells, Howland, Barton and Albany, lay outside the city limits at the time, and a statute of the Ontario Legislature was needed to qualify it as the site for a Toronto cathedral. Sweatman negotiated this step, and he arranged a purchase of the lands from a syndicate of businessmen who had scooped up the property from the original owners, the Wells family. The syndicate, it was said, "offered the site on very favourable terms."

The choice of an architect to design the new St. Alban's seems not to have been a problem. He was Richard Windeyer, best known for his Second Empire style Post Office Building on Adelaide Street at the top of Toronto Street. As a model for his cathedral, Windeyer looked to the original St. Alban's in Hertfordshire; it was an outstanding example of Norman architecture with an outside length of 550 feet and a nave of 292 feet. Windeyer wasn't operating on such a mammoth scale, but his ambitions were fierce, and so were his work habits and those of his contractors. They began construction on August 20, 1885, and before the year was out, a small part of the structure, roofed and fitted, was available for a correspondingly small congregation to hold services. Eighteen months later,

the building had reached sixteen feet in height, and on June 16, 1887, the proud con-
ceiver of the whole enterprise, the Venerable Arthur Sweatman, laid the corner-
stone of the Choir. Another two and a half years on, the Crypt was completed,
and in November 1889, regular services began at St. Alban the Martyr.

That may have been St. Alban's most triumphant moment. Its history
was not all downhill from there, but neither did it come close to the
hopes and plans that Archbishop Sweatman and the congregation
imagined to be the cathedral's due. The building as it stood in 1889
was in the form it retains in essence to this day: one quarter done,
lacking the 135-foot tower that was fundamental to Windeyer's
design, without the trappings of a fully completed cathedral.

It was the general economic trouble of the 1890s that first interrupted work on the structure, and in the following decades, every
time the Anglican leaders cranked up the ambition to nudge the construction in the direction of completion, something got in the way. In
1909, Archbishop Sweatman died, depriving the cathedral of his force
of leadership. Two years later, Sir Henry Pellatt, who was erecting his
own lavish digs at Casa Loma a few blocks north of St. Alban's, took
charge of the building campaign. A well-regarded American architect,
Ralph Cram, was hired — Windeyer died in 1900 — but Cram's redesign
never got far from the drawing board largely because the Anglican construction budget was deflected to cover the cost of the new St. Paul's Church on
Bloor Street East. At that point, the First World War halted further thoughts of building. Sir Henry, burdened with his own financial problems at Casa Loma, was compelled
to step aside from the cathedral project, and some years afterwards, in the late 1920s, the
interior of the church itself suffered damage in a sudden fire. St. Alban's, once the
Anglican favourite son, was now the Anglican orphan, and in 1936, it was reduced in status from cathedral to simple parish church.

An historian of St. James on King Street, writing of poor St. Alban's fate, offered a
blunt summing up: "The vision...of a self-governing, self-financing and self-controlled

*The Most Reverend Arthur
Sweatman was the driving
force behind the building
of St. Alban's Cathedral in
the 1880s.*

corporation devoted to the service of a Diocese as a whole…was what had failed St. Alban's after fifty years of blundering." The writer was in a position to have been more charitable in his assessment, since it was St. James that, in 1936, ascended to the cherished title of cathedral of the Diocese, but he seems to have written nothing less than the painful truth about the mismanagement that had doomed St. Alban's.

Still, St. Alban's had much to be proud of in its history and in its physical presence. It loomed above Howland Avenue and the other nearby streets in massive authority, unexpected in the surroundings, built primarily of brownish-red sandstone from the Credit Valley that, in changing weather, sometimes took on a glorious purple hue and at other times appeared to be a haunting grey. Just to the north, facing on Howland, stood the See House, official residence for the archbishop, a graceful brick home designed in Queen Anne style by Toronto architects Darling & Pearson. A few steps further north, the church put up a plain brick building that was intended as a chapel for daily services but that came to serve many purposes, including a period from 1898 to 1910 when it was occupied by St. Alban's Cathedral Boys School under the mastership of Marmaduke Matthews of nearby Wychwood.

Despite St. Alban's failure to reach physical completion, its congregation remained large and constant until World War II. Then the postwar change in demographics in the neighbourhoods closest to the church led inexorably to the end of full pews on Sunday mornings at St. Alban's. The original Anglo-Saxon residents of the Annex, many of them Anglican parishioners, moved to the suburbs and were replaced by immigrants from continental Europe who made unlikely candidates for the Anglican faith. Religion in general counted for much less in Torontonians' lives, and the former cathedral on Howland, incomplete and often empty of activities, grew more anachronistic and forlorn.

The long process of a more secular resurgence began in 1964 with the arrival on the church premises of St. George's College. It was a new school for boy choristers, and during the week, it rented at bargain rates the vacant St. Alban's buildings, which it converted to classrooms and rehearsal quarters. (The lovely See House became the college offices.) The church continued to offer Sunday services, but over the next couple of decades, as St. George's grew large and thriving, it became apparent to the school and to the Diocese

Timothy Eaton's money contributed to the erection in 1887 of Trinity Methodist Church, now Trinity-St. Paul's United, on Bloor Street West.

When Trinity Methodist opened its doors, it accommodated 2,000 parishioners, making it the largest Protestant church in Canada at the time.

that St. George's should assume proprietorship of the entire St. Alban's property, church and all. The only people who resisted the sale were the members of the ever dwindling St. Alban's congregation. The sale discussions often disintegrated into testy quarrels and dragged on for a dozen years until 2000, when the Diocese at last put its foot down. St. Alban's was sold to St. George's at a fair price, and the remaining St. Alban's parishioners moved their place of Sunday worship to St. Mathias Church a few blocks south. At the time, the last St. Alban's congregation — those parishioners who had opposed the sale of the church for years and were the final representatives of the optimistic Anglican legions of Bishop Sweatman a century earlier — consisted of a mere six stubborn souls.

St. George's launched itself on a scrupulous refurbishing of St. Alban's interior, and in the process, many fine pieces of decor were uncovered beneath the ruin of the 1920s fire and the hasty repairs of the time that had covered over the damage. The discoveries included a large band of lovely stencilling, probably dating from 1910, that ran just below the roof line. In the beauty of the restoration, St. George's resident pastor now conducts chapel for the school's boys each weekday morning, twice on Wednesdays, plus Friday evensong. But St. Alban's, the unfinished building that was once the cathedral of the Anglican Diocese, remains quiet on Sundays.

Walmer Road Baptist Church, built in 1888, was for years Canada's biggest Baptist church, holding 1,500 worshippers.

THE FIRST GOOD WORKS for the community that the Annex's early and wealthy residents performed was to put up churches. Trinity Methodist Church on the south side of Bloor at Robert Street was largely financed by Timothy Eaton and his newly settled fellow Annex homeowners of the merchant and manufacturing classes. The architectural firm of Edmund Burke and Henry Langley designed and erected the building in 1887 in a resounding Richardsonian-Romanesque style to seat 2,000 parishioners, a capacity that made it for years Canada's largest Protestant church. Burke & Langley were also the architects of Walmer Road Baptist Church which likewise went up in the late 1880s and which owed much of its financing to the Harris side of the Massey Harris agricultural equipment company. The church's principal founder and first minister was the Reverend Elmore Harris of that family, and the church itself, built to accommodate 1,500, was the country's largest place of Baptist worship at the time of its completion. The Annex's Presbyterians found their home in Bloor Street Presbyterian Church at the corner of Huron Street, designed in 1889 by the architect William Gregg in a Gothic revival style. At the time of the 1925 church reform, which joined Presbyterians, Methodists and Congregationalists under the umbrella of the United Church, the names of Trinity Methodist and Huron Presbyterian were changed to Trinity United (now Trinity-St. Paul's United) and Huron Street United. This was an event that didn't altogether please Huron Street's often controversial minister of the time, the Reverend George Pidgeon, nor 240 of its members — out of a total congregation of 1,366 — who walked out, never to return.

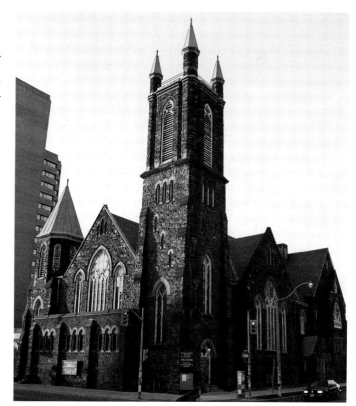

Constructed in 1889, Bloor Street Presbyterian Church (now Bloor Street United) was largely financed by the Harris family of the Massey Harris farm equipment company.

Other less mainstream religions also set up shop in the Annex. The First Church of Christian Science was one, building a church at the northwest corner of St. George and Lowther in 1916 that, in the Christian Science fashion, didn't look much like a church. Somewhat later, the Quakers took over an exceptionally handsome redbrick house at Bedford and Lowther, once the home of the lawyer Miller Lash, and converted it to the Society of Friends Meeting House. Christian fundamentalists got a small piece of the Annex, building the New Apostolic Church on Dupont. Baha'i converted a lovely old home on Huron just north of Bloor into a centre for its faith. And the Tibetan Buddhists went into operation in a more humble but colourful little house on Madison, also close to Bloor.

OF ALL THE INSTITUTIONS of mind, spirit and soul that have made their homes in the Annex, the one that caused most consternation among other Annex citizens wasn't a religion but rather something closer to a psychological cult. It operated as a non-medical lay organization offering group therapy to its members, and it was the brainchild of a woman named Lea Hindley-Smith who called her creation Therafields. At the height of the Therafields phenomenon in the 1970s, Smith claimed 800 members throughout Toronto, and of those, at least 200 lived in twenty Therafields-owned Annex homes that were worth close to five million dollars on the real estate market. These were numbers that came to strike fear into the hearts of many Annex residents. (The Therafields enterprise, which was administered from an office building on Dupont west of Spadina, also included a farm in the Caledon hills, four other rural houses and two Florida properties.)

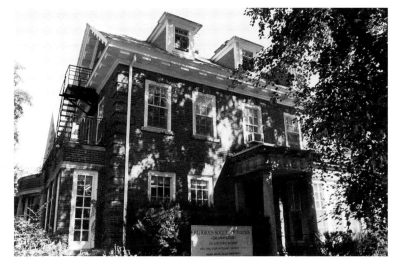

The former residence of a prominent Toronto lawyer named Miller Lash, the house at Lowther and Bedford is now the Society of Friends Meeting House providing Quakers with a gathering place.

Lea Hindley-Smith was Welsh-born, middle-aged and plump, with a towering, blond bouffant hairdo. She had no formal training in psychiatry when she surfaced in the Annex in 1962, but she possessed a formidable presence, an unbreachable sense of conviction, and the germ of a good idea. Her notion was that individual therapy — the classic one-to-one relationship between therapist and patient — might be ultimately destructive for young single patients who moved between the contact of therapy and the isolation of their one-person homes and apartments. Mrs. Smith advocated that it would be far better to gather alienated people into groups in shared accommodations where, under her guidance as therapist, all could air and analyze their problems in a supportive atmosphere for both individual and group therapy.

Over the following years, Smith found many takers for her proposition. She bought two or three heavily mortgaged Annex houses into which her patient-followers moved, and as the group expanded into more houses, she trained the most keen of her followers to

OPPOSITE: Christian Science made its home in the Annex when it opened the First Church of Christian Science on St. George Street in 1916.

The Baha'i faith established itself in a lovely late-nineteenth-century house on Huron Street.

upgrade to the therapist level. Therafields got a major boost at its beginnings when the Reverend Gregory Baum, an influential Catholic theologian at St. Michael's College, endorsed the Smith techniques. His approval was instrumental in steering priests and nuns who were experiencing difficulties with their vocations into the Therafields fold. One ex-seminarian named Thomas O'Sullivan married Mrs. Smith's daughter and became a therapist second only in prestige to Mrs. Smith. Even after O'Sullivan and the daughter divorced, he remained a key Therafields therapist and a director of the corporation that ran the mini-empire of therapy.

The deal for Therafields' live-in members seems to have been remarkably one-way in financial terms. Ownership of the houses was registered in the names of Therafield company entities, and in return for accommodation in one of the houses, often two people per bedroom, members paid rent, bought and cooked food in a communal arrangement, handed over a fee for therapy, and supplied the labour for each house's upkeep. The latter included everything from fashioning the macrame and wall hangings that were the inevitable choice in decor to managing larger renovations. Some members taught themselves carpentry, others took a hand at plastering or plumbing or wiring. And all members were expected to devote part of their evenings and weekends, at no remuneration, to slicking up the old houses. It was a system that meant that the corporate Therafields had the potential to benefit in the long run from the rise in house values provided by the members' no-cost labours.

By the early 1970s, most Annex residents were aware of Therafields' incursions on to Admiral and Walmer and Brunswick and a couple of other streets where it bought several houses on each block. But the alarm bells rang loudest when Therafields put together a cluster of contiguous houses on Brunswick and Kendal. Therafields called this arrangement a "milieu," an important step toward the ideal of a self-contained community exclusive to Therafields members. Real-estate speculators, who regarded consecutive single-ownership properties as a guaranteed fortune-maker, had another name for them:

"assemblies." And when Therafields got its hands on five houses on Brunswick (numbers 477 through 485) that backed on an eight-suite apartment building and a house on Kendal (numbers 68-70 and 72), it confirmed its status as the largest assembler of land in the Annex. That was when the Brunswick neighbours went into panic mode.

The neighbours took the matter of the Brunswick-Kendal assembly to the Ontario Municipal Board. Their purpose at the OMB wasn't to upset Therafields' purchase of the houses, though they wouldn't have objected to such a result. The principal aim was to flush Therafields into the open where the neighbours could examine its intentions for Brunswick and Kendal. Would Therafields, which seemed disturbingly close-mouthed and shadowy to the rest of the Annex, act in a manner that qualified as community-minded? What were its plans for all those houses? Might Therafields tear them down and apply for city permission to erect a large and intrusive structure covering all the properties? For all anyone knew, Therafields' operations may have been legitimate and benign, but the Annex people were looking for answers to their questions.

None was provided at the OMB hearings. Since Therafields had so far done nothing except buy houses, they had broken no bylaw and committed no act that called for policing by the Municipal Board or other government agencies. As a legal issue, Therafields' assembly of the Brunswick-Kendal houses drifted away, but the episode deepened the distrust that Annex residents felt for Mrs. Smith's organization. To many, there was something creepy about all the men and women, mostly in their twenties and thirties, who lived in the Therafields houses, coming and going in silent groups, often switching living quarters from one Annex house to another, phantoms to the rest of the homeowners in the neighbourhood. What was more unsettling for the Annex was the power that Therafields represented with its significant numbers in home

In the 1990s, Tiber Buddhists announced their Annex presence when they decorated the house at 11 Madison with flags, symbols and lots of yellow paint.

The woman with the awesome bouffant is Lea Hindley-Smith, founder of a cult-like therapeutic community that struck fear into the Annex for almost three decades. The man is her companion, Visvaldis Upenieks.

ownership and in tenants who were also voters wielding possible political clout. This attitude of suspicion and distrust deepened over the following decade as Therafields went about its mysterious business.

In the end, which arrived in the mid-1980s, the demise of Therafields came in anticlimactic fashion. Nothing that Annex residents precipitated was a factor in bringing down the organization. It self-destructed on its own with help from Toronto's real estate tumult of the period. In part, the problem was that Lea Hindley-Smith's concept — Mrs. Smith had retreated to Florida in the 1970s to write a double trilogy of fiction cum biography titled *The Summonsa Tapestries* — proved not to hold up over the long haul. Philip McKenna, a Catholic theologian who became a leading Therafields therapist, later described the Smith organization as "a not very well thought-out attempt at creating a community." But more than something innate in Therafields, it was the group housing strategy that caused its demise. In purchasing Annex properties by the dozens, Therafields overextended itself to the breaking point, and when the real estate market tumbled in the early 1980s, with interest on first mortgages rising to a staggering seventeen percent, Therafields was forced into ruinous sales. And in an unfortunate irony for the organization, astute buyers took note of the amateur renovation jobs performed by Therafields' self-taught plumbers and carpenters and scaled back the purchase prices.

After the sell-off of the Therafields realty, many of its former therapists continued to practise under other auspices. Philip McKenna joined with some ex-Therafieldians in a new therapeutic group called CTP. "Our strong academic component was corrective of our Therafields formation," McKenna has written of CTP, "but the central place of therapy groups was a retrieval of what was best in Therafields." As a physical entity, however, the organization whose large real estate holdings generated turmoil in the Annex for two decades vanished without a trace.

On weekends, members of Therafields retreated from the group's Annex homes to a farm in Caledon for marathon therapy sessions.

CHAPTER FIVE

School Days, School Days

THE GIRLS IN THE blue tunics and blazers, the long black stockings, and the blue berets with the letters SMC embroidered in red across the front looked as if they might have stepped from the illustrations for the Ludwig Bemelman's children's book, *Madeline:*

> In an old house in Paris
> that was covered with vines
> lived twelve little girls in two straight lines.

Except that the girls in the blue tunics and blazers were filing through the streets of the Annex, not of Paris, and there were about twenty-five of them, double the twelve in *Madeline*. They were the boarders of St. Mildred's College, and each morning after breakfast, rain or snow, sunny or freezing, the Anglican Sisters who administered the school walked the girls up and down Brunswick, Barton, Kendal and the other streets of the west Annex, then back to the school at 36 Walmer on the southwest corner of Lowther to join the day girls — there were close to 100 of them — for classes in every level from kindergarten to grade thirteen.

The Anglican Community of the Sisters of the Church, an English order established in the 1870s, founded St. Mildred's in 1891 and moved it to the Walmer address in 1908.

The head girl (sitting in the centre) and prefects of St. Mildred's College in 1952. The school stood at the southwest corner of Lowther and Walmer from 1908 to 1969. Dress code: the hem of each girl's tunic had to be no more than four inches above the knee when kneeling for measurement.

The first Huron Street Public School was built, over the objections of wealthy Annex neighbours, in 1889 and stood until its demolition in 1956. This photo dates from the mid-1890s.

Number 36 embraced two red stone Victorian mansions eventually joined in the middle by a small modern gymnasium. Most of the teaching was handled by women from outside the order, but the Sisters ran the school and cared for the boarders, who were as young as seven and who were permitted to go home only every other Saturday and to receive family visits for just one hour each week.

To the girls, the Sisters were figures of mystery and humour. They wore layers of billowing black clothing from the hidden pockets of which they could produce on request a myriad of objects — a pen, a knitting needle, a small book. The school principal was always chosen from among the Sisters, and perhaps the most admired of the principals was Sister Thurza whose tenure extended into the 1940s. She was a tomboyish, practical woman who had many brothers, and she instilled in her students a love of reading and a strong ethical sense, even about premarital sex. "Do not bring your husband second-hand love," she warned the girls.

In 1962, the Board of Governors of the Lightbourn School in Oakville, likewise all girls, invited the Sisters of the Church to administer Lightbourn. Six years later, the two schools entered into a formal amalgamation, St. Mildred's-Lightbourn School, situated in Oakville. In the late spring of 1968, the Sisters moved from the Annex, first selling the property at Walmer and Lowther to a developer for a handsome sum. Where once the girls in the blue tunics and blazers had received their education from the women in the flowing black garments, there was now erected a plain ten-storey apartment building.

IN THE ANNEX'S HISTORY, it has been home to one public elementary school for Annex children, Huron Street Public School, and to at least a score of independent or fees-paying schools that catered almost entirely to children from beyond the Annex. Some of the private schools later moved and flourished elsewhere in the manner of St. Mildred's, and some in time closed shop altogether. Havergal College, the exclusive school for girls, was one of the former, beginning in the Annex before it moved to much larger quarters on Avenue Road in north Toronto. Miss Veales' School for Young Ladies on Bedford Road in the early twentieth century was one of the schools that vanished; its demise probably had

Huron School's fashionably dressed kindergarten teachers posed with their cat on an Annex porch in 1895.

nothing to do with the incident when Flora Eaton lost control of her electric runabout while turning off Bloor on to Bedford and flattened the ornamental gates to the Veales establishment. Several other independent Annex schools, unlike St. Mildred's, Havergal and Miss Veales, remain in place today. These schools have added youth and liveliness to the neighbourhood, but this is not to say that the Annex has invariably welcomed such institutions with open arms.

In the 1920s, the residents of Prince Arthur Avenue went to extravagant measures to keep one interloping school off their street. The expensive fuss began in the spring of 1921 when St. Basil's, a boys school in the Roman Catholic Separate School system, was evicted

Huron's junior students took their classes outdoors on this balmy spring day in 1895.

from its building on St. Vincent Street (a non-Annex thoroughfare) to make way for a road improvement. As a replacement, the Separate School Board bought two adjoining houses on Prince Arthur, numbers 14 and 18, a total of 124 feet in frontage. The plan was to carry out two simultaneous steps: move the boys of St. Basil's to classes in the two houses soon after the Board took possession of the properties on August 19, 1921, and make the necessary structural changes that would convert the buildings into a proper schoolhouse. At the time of the purchase, number 14 was vacant and number 18 operated as a boardinghouse. These circumstances indicated that Prince Arthur might have been coming down in the world from its previously lofty status as an enclave of privilege, but there remained a majority of well-to-do residents on the street who reeled at the notion of adolescents bringing their noise and hormones to Prince Arthur.

The residents included two members of the Gooderham family in two different houses, two physicians, a prominent architect named Henry Sproatt, a University of Toronto professor, and a partner in the highly regarded law firm of Bain, Bicknell, Macdonnell & Gordon. All of these worthy citizens were fast off the mark in letting their unhappiness over St. Basil's be known at City Hall. The politicians were just as swift in taking action to discourage the School Board. On September 22, little more than a month after the Board's purchase of the two houses, City Council passed a bylaw that could not have been more specific; it prohibited the use of "property on either side of Prince Arthur Avenue between Avenue Road and Huron Street for any other purpose than that of a detached private residence." The Board accepted the city's challenge and took it and the new bylaw to court. This meant it was the City of Toronto that carried the financial load of the legal proceedings which lasted over the next four years, though the Prince Arthur residents were vigilant in prodding the politicians to stay the full course through four different levels of court.

The days of the original Huron School building were numbered when this photo was taken post-World War II. The school's annex building on the right was erected in 1915.

The case turned on the interpretation of the Municipal Act and its impact on the bylaw in question, and at trial and in the Ontario Court of Appeal, the city as defendant prevailed. But the Supreme Court of Canada overturned the bylaw and found in favour of the plaintiff School Board. This ruling sent all parties to the body of highest appeal for Canadian cases in those years, the Privy Council in London, England. In July 1925, the

Privy Council ended the protracted squabble by upholding the bylaw's validity and coming down on the side of the city and therefore of the elite of Prince Arthur: St. Basil's had to get off the street. Which it did, moving a few hundred yards east to Hazelton Avenue in Yorkville, where the Board at last built its new school.

The Privy Council ruling didn't bring peace to beleaguered Prince Arthur. The Toronto Orthopedic Hospital, expecting that it would be more welcome on the street with its patients — placid adults who suffered mostly in silence from disintegrating vertebrae and dislocated hips — took an option to purchase numbers 14 and 18 from the School Board for the purpose of erecting a new hospital. Prince Arthur's residents didn't want a hospital any more than they wanted a school. Reluctant to bear the responsibility of litigation all by themselves, they enlisted the support of homeowners in the neighbouring streets. Once again, the residents prevailed in court, and the Separate School Board, conceding the result to be an ultimate defeat, sold the two properties to purchasers who wanted nothing more than to make their homes on Prince Arthur.

A lasting benefit to the Annex that arose out of the tussle over the Orthopedic Hospital was the formation of the Annex Ratepayers Association. This was the name that the Prince Arthur residents and their recruits from the adjoining blocks eventually assumed. The new ARA found other issues at which to take umbrage; the proliferation of boarding houses in the 1930s was one. But the organization remained for many years limited in geographical scope, not welcoming to its membership residents west of Walmer or north of Boswell. The ARA was thus an exclusive outfit in its beginnings, and it suffered blips in continuity, virtually vanishing during World War II. It was also eclipsed by the formation of two other organizations in 1952, the West Annex and East Annex Neighbourhood Associations. But by 1960, the two new groups threw in their lot with the ARA which now covered the full Annex and admitted tenants to membership for the first time. In 1969, the ARA became officially a residents' association (though it didn't change its name to Annex Residents' Association until 1975), and from then on, it displayed activist muscle and took frequently effective stands against invasions by builders of apartment high-rises and proponents of expressways.

A SCHOOL OF EVEN earlier vintage than St. Basil's that wealthy Annex people opposed in the pre-building phase was the one that became the longest lived of them all, Huron Street Public School. Probably because many residents sent their own kids to Upper Canada College and other private schools, they saw only an annoyance in the presence of a public school in their midst. Their opposition, however, never reached serious litigation, and the first Huron School building went up in 1889, three storeys high, maple-paneled rooms inside and, outside,

The contemporary Huron School building, completed in 1957, was in contrast to the original. lower slung, brighter and more hospitable.

a saucy cupola on the roof. In 1915, with school enrolment ever increasing in the district, Huron Street added an annex building that was designed in a style that reflected the taste in many of the surrounding houses with its pleasing Queen Anne features. The original 1889 structure was demolished in 1956, replaced by a building that was, for the times, of a trail-blazing modernity. The new school was lower slung and more immediately hospitable, bright with colour in enduring contrast to the annex building that still remains at the rear of the school property.

THE MOTIVES FOR STARTING the independent schools that found their locations in the Annex seem traditional, honourable and, in some cases, original. Dr. William Blatz had nothing but progressive intentions in mind in 1926 when he became the first director of a centre for child development that flourished as the much admired laboratory school and research facility at 45 Walmer under the name of the Institute of Child Study.

Blatz was born in Hamilton, Ontario, in 1895, and became a pediatrician and a member of the University of Toronto's Department of Psychology. He took on many activities over the years that made him Canada's best-known psychologist. It was Blatz who, in the confusion that followed the birth of the Dionne quintuplets in 1934, was summoned by the Ontario government to organize the girls' daily lives, to test them, study them, plan their play, their discipline (definitely no spanking), their diet, their bowel movements. Later, in the 1950s and 1960s, Blatz, an articulate communicator, was a panelist along with novelist Morley Callaghan and drama critic Nathan Cohen on CBC-TV's immensely popular quiz and opinion show, *Fighting Words*.

Once the home of the lawyer Leighton McCarthy, the mansion at 45 Walmer Road was converted in 1954 to house the progressive primary school called the Institute of Child Study.

But the Institute of Child Study was Blatz's enduring work. It originated in a scheme called the Hart House Muscle Function Re-education Program that was developed at the University of Toronto in 1916 to rehabilitate soldiers wounded during World War I. Psychologists discovered, not surprisingly, that the soldier patients recovered best if they became active and independent participants in their own training program. In the mid-1920s, the psychologists set out to bring the same approach to preschool children and hired Blatz to mastermind the project. Blatz began with eight kids from ages two to four, applying to them the ideas explored by the Hart House team. What eventually emerged from these beginnings, in the words of today's ICS staff, was "a program based on a general philosophy of education which recognizes the holistic, active nature of the children, nurturing their natural curiosity and creativity."

The notion caught on among Toronto parents who thought the Blatz approach offered their kids a better shot at an effective education. By 1954, when the ICS was established in business to stay, the school bought the large house at 45 Walmer, and with an enrolment of almost 200 children from kindergarten to grade six, it has become best known as the school where parents with the resources — $6,000 per kid per year — send their sons and daughters for teaching that grew in large part from the techniques pioneered by William Blatz.

THE URGE TO LAUNCH Royal St. George's College on Howland Avenue derived from a summer school and camp for young choral singers at St. James Cathedral in the early 1960s. The camp brought such satisfaction to the men in charge of it that they wanted to freeze the joy and accomplishment of the experience in a more permanent institution. Anglican chorister schools — where boys got both conventional schooling and intense instruction in the vocal arts — had been a part of the education system in Britain for centuries but were unknown in Canada in the 1960s. The men from the St. James camp formed a scheme to fill the void.

The key players included Jack Wright, then the head of the junior school at St. Andrew's College in Aurora, Ontario, and John Bradley, an accomplished organist and choirmaster. They and the others who were keen to press the idea of a chorister school to reality were fortuitously joined by the Reverend Ken Scott, the rector at St. Alban's Church who, at that waning stage of the church's history, had plenty of space on his hands and not much to put in it. In September 1964, the fledgling chorister school, called St. George's (without, as yet, the "Royal"), moved into part of St. Alban's premises. Jack Wright served as the principal, John Bradley handled the choir, the Rev. Scott taught some subjects, and the school consisted that first year of grades 7 and 8.

Two young scholars from St. George's College hurry down Howland Avenue to classes shortly after the school opened in 1964.

The enterprise succeeded on all levels: academic, musical, financial. In the latter category, St. Alban's charged only minimal rent for facilities that included a church with all the acoustical advantages that suited a choir. From this monetary head start, St. George's steadily added new grades above and below the original 7 and 8. (Today, with 430 students, the school covers grades 3 through 12.) And the school choir acquired such an impressive artistic reputation that it toured much of the world, performing in Europe, Japan and most parts of North America. With each year of its existence, St. George's approached the ideal that its founders had in mind. The choir was of showpiece status, and the music program expanded to embrace instrumental groups, classics and jazz, from Wolfgang Amadeus Mozart to Miles Davis. But at the same time, academic excellence together with the busy round of extracurricular activities customary to independent boys' schools turned into perhaps St. George's chief drawing card.

As for the "Royal" in the school's name, it appears to have resulted from an error on the part of Buckingham Palace. In the early 1980s, St. George's learned that the Toronto French School had asked for and received Elizabeth II's agreement to serve as a Patron of the school. This sounded like something that would suit St. George's, and its then Chairman of the Board, John Latimer, who later became the school's third principal, made the appropriate application. Latimer knew his way around such matters since he was working at the time in the Office of Protocol at Queen's Park. But somewhere in the Buckingham Palace bureaucracy, the St. George's application generated a misunderstanding, and in due course, the school received from the Palace, not word that the Queen would be a Patron, but official permission for St. George's to designate itself as "Royal." This was not what the school had requested, and the Board of Governors entered into a ferocious debate over the wisdom of accepting the mistaken designation. The ultimate decision was that the school would appear impolite, and maybe downright offensive to Her Majesty, in declining the erroneous honour. Hence, the school became Royal St. George's College.

JAMES PLINY WHITNEY, a Conservative and a lawyer from Morrisburg in eastern Ontario, led his party to power in the province in 1905, becoming himself the premier, on a platform

of elevating Ontario education from the lamentable level on which it was stuck. Whitney's program began with an upgrade in teaching. A report that he commissioned from his Ministry of Education put the problem in perspective. "Today we must pay the man who splits our wood at least $1.50 a day; we can get a teacher — a poor one at that — at less than a dollar a day." To make teaching a better paying proposition and to eliminate the ill-equipped teachers who didn't mind working for less than a wood-splitter's wage, Whitney ordered the introduction of institutions, previously unknown in Ontario, that taught teachers how to teach. In the first years of his new government, the Ministry of Education opened four model schools for the instruction of elementary school teachers, and it led the initiative at the University of Toronto for a Faculty of Education that became the training

The University of Toronto Schools opened on September 12, 1910, at the southeast corner of Bloor and Spadina, designated by the province as the school where teachers-in-training practised their pedagogical skills.

ground for secondary school teachers. It was the opening of the faculty that led in a round-about fashion to the school called the University of Toronto Schools.

Once the university had a Faculty of Education to play with, it conceived a need for "practice schools." These were defined as secondary schools with students who would comprise captive audiences on whom the teachers in training could hone their skills. The university announced a grand plan: 200 student teachers at the Faculty of Education and 1,200 secondary-level students in two practice schools, one for boys and one for girls. By the time the Ministry of Education finished crunching numbers, it concluded that the sum it could put into the faculty and the practice schools was $175,000. This was a generous enough figure but not enough to meet the university's grand projections, which were thus scaled back to include just one practice school of only 350 students who would all be boys. The promise was that a similar school for girls would come later; its eventual existence was recognized in theory in the name of the boys' school, "University of Toronto Schools" in the plural. But for reasons of economics and inertia, the practice school for girls never got past the theory stage, and girls would not enter the UTS picture until 1973 when the all-boy UTS went coeducational.

In 1910, a building to house both the Faculty of Education and UTS was erected at the southeast corner of Bloor and Spadina. It was a stalwart structure, three storeys high and constructed of brick and terra cotta. The Faculty occupied the building's west half, UTS classrooms were in the east half, and for the boys of this new and experimental school, no expense was spared in equipment. The chemistry and physics rooms were stocked with top-of-the-line material imported at a cost of $25,000 from England; the plumbing alone in the labs came at $4,000. The staff received equally royal treatment. The first principal, Henry Job Crawford, a classics specialist nick-named "the Bull" by the boys, was classified at the status and pay of a University of Toronto associate professor, and his fifteen meticulously recruited teachers were paid as much as $2,500 a year, which put them at the upper limits of 1910 remuneration for teachers. For the parents of the boys, who numbered 374 in UTS's opening year, the cost of education at the spiffy school was twenty dollars per term for three terms, "payable in advance."

The students of UTS in the workshop, 1915: all male, all white, virtually all Protestant.

From the start, since it was intended as a practice school, UTS tolerated no intellectual slackers among its boys. "Our ideal," said Robert Falconer, the University of Toronto president at the time, "has been to show the teachers-in-training what a first-class school should be." But almost immediately, academic excellence became a hallmark of the school by itself and without reference to its status as a practice school. The UTS teachers were superior to those at other schools, the expectations placed on its students more demanding, and the results more satisfying and measured in marks scored on examinations and in scholarships won to universities.

UTS became the destination of choice among parents, almost entirely middle and upper middle class, who wanted access for their sons to the city's best available education.

Not all parents got their wish. By 1914, as the numbers of UTS applicants climbed, the school introduced an entrance exam that eliminated boys who probably couldn't keep the academic pace. (The entrance exam remains in effect today; slightly fewer than 1,000 applicants write it, and about a tenth of them survive the final cut.) Under Henry "the Bull" Crawford and his successors, even boys who passed the exam weren't guaranteed a permanent place at the school. John Ross Robertson, the legendary publisher of the Telegram and a force of much influence in Toronto, sent his nephew and ward, George Holland, to UTS in its early years. "The concentration so necessary to progress seems quite beyond George," Crawford soon wrote to Robertson in a letter that left little doubt of its purpose. Robertson withdrew George and enrolled him at Upper Canada College.

At first glance, the UTS of its first half century might have been confused with UCC and other private schools. The boys were required to wear jackets and ties, the cadet corps was compulsory, the principal was called "head master" and the teachers were "masters." But UTS had neither the physical plant — no sports grounds to call its own — nor the mindset of the usual private school. UTS was the sort of place where students with unconventional interests — Keynesian economics, bebop, Lepidoptera — were regarded as the norm and where the competition for top marks was zesty and even cutthroat.

"One thing UTS education accomplished," the poet Dennis Lee, class of 1957, said in his valedictory speech, "was to throw us into the midst of a great number of new ideas. I don't think anyone could stay out of the constant flow of discussions and arguments."

In the early 1970s, UTS began a long process of overhaul. Girl students and women teachers arrived. Though this move came over the dead bodies of many alumni, the male-female school was achieved with a maximum of speedy harmony at the student and teacher levels. The only casualties were the football and hockey teams, which, once a school pride, were discontinued without enough male students to fill out the team rosters. The cadet corps likewise vanished. So did the jackets and ties and the Tom Brown School Days nomenclature, "head master" and "master." The school's original purpose as a practice school for teachers in training was rethought (the teachers began to practise on students at a broader spectrum of high schools), and the Faculty of Education itself moved elsewhere, leaving the Bloor Street building to UTS, which expanded its enrolment to fill

the empty spaces. The number of students rose to 640 by the twenty-first century, and after the provincial government withdrew most of its funding for UTS in the early 1990s, the annual fees for each student climbed into five-figure territory. The ethnic and racial background of the students altered too, and UTS was no longer the place of predominantly WASP boys and girls that it had been for most of its existence. But, amid the massive changes, the defining attribute of the school remained consistent: UTS was still a school for smart kids.

The students of UTS, 2001: male and female, multi-cultural, multi-racial.

CHAPTER SIX

Green Space

TORONTO'S EARLY MEN OF PROPERTY were generous in donating land for city parks in which their fellow Torontonians might enjoy the green and open spaces. In 1876, the architect John Howard turned over to the city a whopping 165 acres, which became the brilliant and immense High Park. Downtown, where land was tighter, Goldwin Smith parted with the front lawn of his famous house, the Grange, and the land formed the leafy Grange Park. That gift occurred in 1912, and thirteen years later, Sir Edmund Osler gave the city a small corner of his prime Rosedale property, which emerged as the park called Craigleigh Gardens.

The Annex has had little luck with such gift-givers. The one tiny presentation of Annex property to the city occurred on September 10, 1881, when the Toronto Diocese of the Anglican Church donated an incidental parcel of land, just .689 of an acre in size, for park purposes. The parcel abutted St. Alban's Cathedral on the south, reaching a couple of dozen yards to Barton, and from east to west, it covered the block from Howland to Albany. St. Alban's Square, as it was named, formed a civilized pause in the midst of the streets and buildings, and much later in its history, in 1997, the park acquired an additional small flourish in its northwest corner with the creation by the environmental group, Grassroots Albany, of Jacobs' Ladder. The Ladder consists of a few hardy rosebushes planted against a wrought-iron fence, and it offers a salute to one of the neighbourhood's favourite residents, Jane Jacobs of Albany Avenue, the influential writer about cities.

Part of the reason why there were no further gifts of Annex property to serve as parkland, why no equivalent of the donations of Howard or Smith or Osler emerged on St. George or

In 1906, the City of Toronto purchased an acre of land in the midst of a housing development in the west Annex, converted it to parkland, and named it Kendal Square. The name stuck for fifty years.

Walmer, was that the Annex had just enough land, with none left over, to accommodate all the houses that Simeon Janes and the other profit-driven developers allowed for in their plans of subdivision. In explaining themselves, the developers pointed out the proximity of the Annex to the central city's most abundant park, the one outside the Ontario Legislature. With Queen's Park at the doorstep, the reasoning went, who need-

In a corner of St. Alban's Square, the environmental group Grassroots Albany has fashioned a tribute, Jacob's Ladder, to a distinguished neighbourhood resident, author Jane Jacobs.

ed more green space? All of which meant that, over the years, the few and modest parks that lie within Annex borders have been the product of the city's own actions, the insistence of the Annex Residents' Association, and of bits of serendipitous good fortune.

The Bloor subway line, completed in 1966, generated parkettes on the property that the city expropriated for construction purposes. Not all of the parkettes were successful, and of the ones that turned into successes, not all were long lived. The Joseph Burr Tyrell Parkette between Brunswick and Dalton is one of the former, tending to be gloomy and uninviting for most of its existence. Ecology Park was one of the latter, an inspired use of property for experimental and educational purposes during its short period of existence from 1987 to 1993. Pollution Probe, the environmental organization, converted the land next to the Spadina subway station into a bountiful garden of native plants that conveyed the message that environmentally correct growth — supplying energy, food, improved quality of air and water — was possible in the middle of the city. Ecology Park was dismantled in 1993 to make way for transportation progress in the form of the Spadina LRT line. But a happy ending may yet emerge in the story of Ecology Park because, in the first years of the twenty-first century, a consortium of the ARA, the Jewish Community Centre and other concerned parties were laying plans to reconstitute the park on the barren lot left behind at the completion of the LRT construction.

St Alban's Square comprises .689 of an acre of parkland donated to the city by the Toronto Diocese of the Anglican Church in 1881.

OPSITE: *Taddle Creek Park, a leafy oasis on Bedford Road, emerged from a struggle in the 1970s between the Annex Residents' Association and a developer who planned to build townhouses on the site.*

Another space over the Bloor subway line, the Albany Parkette on Albany a few yards north of Bloor, represents an additional small victory for the environmentalists. In its early years, despite the water fountain and the tiled chess tables with chairs for players and kibitzers that dress up the tiny piece of land it occupies, the Albany Parkette fell into the category of abused spaces. By day, high school kids and men sipping from bottles in brown paper bags treated the parkette as their personal dumping ground. By night, the strange play of shadows made the place seem too scary to risk using even as a hasty shortcut from the Bathurst subway station at the rear. But in 1998 and 1999, the ARA and Royal St. George's College collaborated in planting two separate gardens encompassing sixty meadow and native plants. While the gardens, which were given the user-friendly name of Where Edges Meet, didn't entirely redeem the parkette from the continuing detritus left by the kids and the outdoor drinkers, it still offered a hint of hope for better days to come.

The otherwise unpromising Albany Parkette is enlivened by two small gardens called Where Edges Meet that encompass sixty meadow and native plants.

The ARA's most notable triumph in the creation of parks is represented by Taddle Creek Park at Bedford and Lowther. If a property development company named Parcon had had its way in 1964, Taddle Creek's land would now be occupied by high rises or townhouses. Parcon's first plan was to erect two apartment towers on Prince Arthur and Lowther west of Bedford. As a sweetener, the developer offered to leave room for a public parkette at the base of the towers. The ARA held out for something more grand than a mere parkette, and to that purpose, it led a sustained charge against the development that lasted for almost two decades. The struggle over the land generated a bitter and divisive debate in city council, and called for a hearing before the

Ontario Municipal Board. During the acrimony, the developer built one nineteen-storey tower on Prince Arthur, but the lot on Lowther remained behind wooden fences, empty and desolate, until the ARA at last came out the winner in the battle. The end was realized in 1976 when the city cut a deal with the developer, a deal that turned the Lowther site into Taddle Creek Park, which came with a fountain, a huge sandbox, a picnic table, benches, slides, swings and all the trimmings.

MUCH EARLIER IN THE Annex's history, the city made a similarly bold move in the interest of providing the neighbourhood with parkland. This occurred in 1906 when City Council interrupted the development of housing on the former Baldwin family property west of Spadina Road and purchased the empty lots which were locked in by four streets, Kendal, Barton, Brunswick and the last short block of Bernard. The land added up to exactly one acre, though a later remeasurement added another .22 of an acre, and the pleasant little oasis was declared a city park available to the neighbouring residents in need of a respite in the open air.

The modest park was given a modest name, Kendal Square, but that changed fifty years later, on November 5, 1956, when the City of Toronto's Board of Control, the ultimate level of city government at the time, voted in favour of a new name for the park: Jean Sibelius Square in honour of the famous Finnish composer. The idea of renaming the park didn't originate with the Board of Control. In fact, the official minutes of the November 5 meeting misspelled Sibelius's first name as "Jan," an error that someone at City Hall caught just before "Jan" was committed to park signs. The initiative for the new name came from the city's Finnish community, which numbered about 6,000, with the majority living in two neighbourhoods, the Beach in the east end and St. Clair-Dufferin in the west end. A Finnish language weekly newspaper, which began publication in 1931, had become a popular success among local Finns. So had an outfit called the Finnish Social Club. The leaders of the community that formed around both entities, reasoning that Sibelius was the Finn best known to non-Finns, chose him as the vehicle for marking the established Finnish presence in Toronto. The Finnish leaders pressed the city for a park — any park — that would henceforth bear Sibelius's name.

The Finns, as it happened, weren't the only citizens of Toronto in the mid-1950s who were keen to put a name to a park. Andrew Janicki, president of the Canadian Polish Congress, wrote to city hall asking that a park or a street or "even a fountain" be

On November 5, 1956, as a result of lobbying by Toronto's Finnish community, the City of Toronto renamed Kendal Square to honour the Finnish composer Jean Sibelius. Hence, Sibelius Square.

To complete the tribute to Jean Sibelius, the Finnish community of Canada donated a sculpture of Sibelius that was unveiled in Sibelius Square on September 30, 1959.

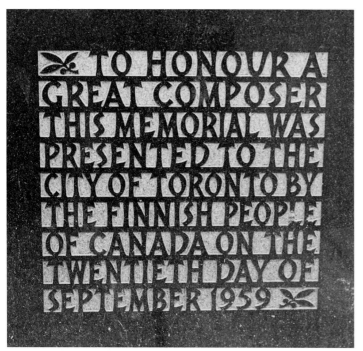

named after Sir Casimir Gzowski, the accomplished Polish-Canadian engineer (and grandfather of the journalist and broadcaster Peter Gzowski). Surpass Petroleums Limited of 77 Victoria Street petitioned that a park be given a name that hailed Sir Winston Churchill. And a member of the Board of Control itself, William R. Allen (whose name was later pinned on the Allen Expressway), politicked to get a park designated in recognition of the works of David A. Balfour, who was a recently retired member of the same Board of Control.

The decision on these proposals and others fell in September 1956 to a three-person subcommittee of the city's Committee on Parks and Exhibitions. At the subcommittee meeting, under the brisk chairmanship of Alderman Kucherepa, a small hitch developed with the Gzowski request when a city hall bureaucrat pointed out that Toronto already had a Casimir Street in salute to the great engineer. But the subcommittee saw this as no impediment to further honours, and the Gzowski application and four others received the subcommittee's approval and the subsequent go-ahead from the Board of Control. One of the other four was the Sibelius application from the Finnish community.

The Kucherepa subcommittee was also responsible for matching parks to applicants. It gave Winston Churchill's name to the park over the reservoir at the corner of St. Clair Avenue and Spadina Road. The Gzowski name went on a new 25-acre park under development in the west end's Sunnyside neighbourhood. Former Controller David Balfour got the biggest park of all, 46.69 acres near Yonge and St. Clair that had formerly been called Reservoir Park. The smallest park, the subcommittee no doubt bearing in mind that the city's Finnish population paled in comparison to Toronto's 40,000 Polish-Canadians, received Jean Sibelius's name.

To celebrate the recognition, the Finnish community staged a small ceremony in the new Jean Sibelius Square on December 6, 1956. The date, chosen deliberately, had resonance for most Finns since it was on December 6, 1917, that Finland won its independence from Russia. On the day of the ceremony in Toronto, Sibelius himself was at home in Finland preparing to mark his ninety-first birthday two days later on December 8. The following year, Sibelius died, and two years after that, on September 20, 1959, the Finnish community arranged another ceremony in Sibelius Square to complete their tribute by unveiling a head and shoulders sculpture of the composer. The sculpture, purchased by Canadian Finns and shipped from Helsinki, was a 1935 work by Vaino Aaltonen, one of Finland's leading artists of the day. At the September 20 event, many of those present grumbled about the placement that the city's park bureaucrats had chosen for the sculpture in the park's northern perimeter. But Aaltonen's piece gave Sibelius a handsome and imposing look, and the head made a commanding presence at the top of a tall shaft of dark marble. While the Sibelius memorial, at the far north side of the park, was hardly the focus of Sibelius Square, it seemed to serve as a galvanizing agent, and in the following years, the park became an active, green and vibrant place.

The poet Dennis Lee once wrote that he found solace in the new beauty of Jean Sibelius Square. At the time, 1968, he lived at 474 Brunswick Avenue across the street from the park, and in his poem, titled "Sibelius Park" (giving it the name which most residents mistakenly called the square), he wrote of a walk home late one afternoon, coming north from Bloor after a hard and sometimes discouraging day of editing at Anansi Press and teaching at Rochdale College. Doubts and questions pulled at him until he reached the last block before home:

> And then Sibelius Park!
>   The grass is wet, it
>   gleams, across the park's wide
>   vista the lanes of ornamental
>   shrub come breathing and the sun has filled the
>   rinsed air till the green goes luminous and it does it
>   does, it comes clear!

WALMER ROAD TRAGEDY AND SOME OF THOSE CONCERNED

CARRIE DAVIES

ERNEST PELLETIER
NEWSBOY.

WHERE Mr MASSEY
WAS SHOT

C. A. MASSEY

Late C. A. Massey of Walmer road, his maid, and the newsboy who witnessed the shooting on the steps of Mr. Massey's home, 169 Walmer road.

✣ CHAPTER SEVEN ✣

Murder!

IT WAS TWENTY MEDIUM paces from the front verandah at 169 Walmer Road to the street, which meant that Bert Massey, retreating down the sidewalk from the verandah in confusion and panic, presented a close target for Carrie Davies, who stood on the verandah itself pointing a loaded Ivor Johnson revolver in Bert's direction.

Second earlier, Carrie had missed Bert with a first shot. She had fired from the open front door as the unsuspecting Bert approached it. Carrie's nervousness and inexperience with guns affected her aim. So did the gloom of the late winter afternoon; the time was 6:25 P.M. on Monday, February 8, 1915. Carrie raised her arm and shot again. This time the bullet caught Bert in the heart, and he dropped to the sidewalk, dead in an instant.

B.K. SANDWELL, THE EDITOR of *Saturday Night* magazine from 1932 to 1951, wrote a famous piece of doggerel: "Toronto has no social classes, Only the Masseys and the masses." C.A. "Bert" Massey was one of those Masseys. He was the grandson of Hart Massey who founded the farm-implement company, Massey-Harris, which generated the family fortune. Bert was the son of Charles Albert Massey, who was the brains behind Massey-Harris's commercial ascendancy, and he was the cousin of Vincent Massey, who would become Canada's first Canadian-born governor general. Alas for Bert, he shared little in the Massey prosperity. His brilliant father died young of typhoid fever in 1884, and when Bert's mother remarried to a humble bank teller, Bert and his siblings were pushed to the fringes of Massey life. Nevertheless, on the $15,000 he inherited from grandfather Hart

In the evening of February 8, 1915, Carrie Davies, a maid at the home of C.A. "Bert" Massey of Walmer Road, shot and killed her employer outside his Walmer Avenue home. Carrie was charged with murder. Vincent Pelletier was delivering newspapers on Walmer at the time of the shooting.

FATHER AND SON

At the moment when Carrie Davies shot Charles A. Massey, known to his friends as "Bert," the Massey son, fourteen-year-old Charlie, was in the basement at the Walmer house working at his glass-blowing hobby. Charlie didn't hear the fatal shot.

and on his own sporadic earnings from a mostly unprofitable business career, Bert could afford the pleasant house on Walmer and a staff consisting of one all-purpose maid. The resident maid in 1915 was eighteen-year-old Carrie Davies.

After the shooting, Carrie closed the front door and went up to her attic bedroom to compose herself. Her mistress, Bert's wife, was in Connecticut visiting her parents, and the couple's only child, fourteen-year-old Charlie, was in the basement working on his glass-blowing hobby. Charlie didn't hear the shot that killed his father.

Sergeant Larry Brown of the Toronto Police, summoned by one of the Walmer neighbours, rushed to the Massey house from the station at few blocks away on London Street. Carrie came down the stairs to meet Brown on the second-floor landing, calm and offering no fuss.

"You see," she said to the sergeant in explanation of the dead man outside, "he ruined my life."

Brown escorted Carrie to City Hall, where she was charged with Bert's murder and locked in a cell to await criminal proceedings.

ANNEX MURDERS ARE SINGULAR. There haven't been many of them, but when they occur, either the crime or the criminal seems to have a one-of-a-kind nature. A man convicted of a 1961 Annex murder became one of the two last people to be executed in Canada; shortly after midnight on December 11, 1962, two men found guilty in two different trials of two different killings were hanged back to back at the Don Jail, and one of the two was the Annex murderer. Another man who is guilty to a certainty in a 1983 Annex murder has never been convicted in a trial because today, many years later, he is still eluding the police despite a search across North America. And yet another Annex murder, which took place in 1994, is routinely referred to in the media as the event that "robbed Toronto of its innocence." This may be an exaggeration, but it is at least true that the murder was the immediate motivation for federal legislation that tightened Canada's immigration laws.

IN NOVEMBER 1961, THERLAND CRATER was hiding out at 116 Kendal Avenue. The Kendal house, which is today handsomely renovated and single family, was then divided into three apartments. Crater was a pimp and drug dealer from Detroit whom that city's police had recruited as the principal witness in the upcoming trial of a Detroit drug king-pin named Gus Saunders on charges of trafficking in heroin. Until the trial date, the cops shipped Crater and his girlfriend, Carolyn Newman, to Toronto to lie low in the second floor apartment of the Kendal house.

Sometime between 6:20 and 6:35 on the morning of November 17, someone entered the house, slit Crater's throat and shot four .38-calibre bullets into his body, then sliced Newman's throat. Almost immediately, Toronto police came up with a suspect in the two murders. He was Arthur Lucas, fifty-four years old, another Detroiter, a man who had worked in his city's pimping business for a couple of decades. Lucas was in Toronto on the night before the murders, staying at the Waverley Hotel on Spadina Avenue not far from the Kendal address. He even admitted he had paid a social call that night on his old hometown pal Therland. But at the time of the murders, Lucas insisted, he was driving back to Detroit. The Toronto cops worked on the theory that Lucas carried out the killings on orders from Gus Saunders to keep Crater off the witness stand in the Saunders trial, and they charged Lucas with two counts of murder.

At Arthur Lucas's trial for Crater's murder in a courtroom at Old City Hall in early May 1962, his defence counsel was a thirty-year-old

Arthur Lucas (middle) was convicted of murdering two people at 116 Kendal Avenue in the early morning of November 17, 1961. He became one of the two last people to be executed in Canada.

Arthur Lucas, brought back from Detroit to face murder charge, with Toronto detectives John Bassett (left) and John Webster.

Ross MacKay (centre) celebrated his call to the Ontario bar in 1957. Five years later, he unsuccessfully defended Arthur Lucas at this murder trial. MacKay himself grew up in the Annex.

lawyer appearing in his first murder trial. His name was Ross MacKay, and coincidentally he had grown up in the Annex, living with his mother at 380A Bloor Street West in a cramped apartment over a variety store. MacKay believed in Lucas's innocence, but he felt the case was stacked against him. He was working on a Legal Aid budget of $800 in fees and expenses; the police and crown spent $40,000 on the prosecution. And in MacKay's opinion, the judge hearing the case, Chief Justice James McRuer of the Ontario Supreme Court, made no effort to conceal in court the enormous revulsion he felt for Lucas, treating him as an alien creature who earned his money in a loathsome profession. The jury seemed to MacKay to be buying into the view of Lucas that McRuer was conveying. "I could tell the jury despised and disbelieved Lucas," MacKay said many years later.

In McRuer's charge to the jury, he devoted fifty-five transcript pages to the case for the prosecution and twenty-two lines to MacKay's case for the defence. McRuer finished his charge at two minutes past one o'clock on the afternoon of May 10, and sent the jurors to the jury room to reach a verdict. They returned to the courtroom at 5:55 that same afternoon with the verdict.

Guilty of capital murder.

On the night of Lucas's execution at the Don Jail, he stood on a trap door in the gallows room with another man who, like Lucas, wore a black hood over his head and a noose around his neck. The second man was Ronald Turpin, twenty-eight years old, convicted of the murder of a Toronto policeman in a shootout on Danforth Avenue in the early hours of February 12, 1962. Turpin's trial took place nineteen days after Lucas's ended and in the same courtroom where Lucas had been convicted. Turpin and Lucas had one other piece of biography in common: both were defended at trial by Ross MacKay.

BRENDAN CARON AND LYNDA KEENAN absorbed the counterculture values of the 1960s, grooving on peace, love and flower power, which explained why they gave their three children such distinctive names: Sharin' Morningstar, Celeste, Summer Sky. It was Sharin', the eldest of the three, nine years old, who went missing on Sunday afternoon, January 23, 1983. The family rented the tidy little house at 493 Dupont Street west of Bathurst, and at 3 P.M. on the 23rd, Lynda left Sharin' at Sibelius Square to play with the neighbourhood kids. Brendan arrived an hour later to walk his daughter home. She was nowhere in sight. The other kids couldn't remember what had happened to Sharin', and by 6:30 P.M., the police were on the search. They called it a missing person case, but the next day, Monday, with no sign of Sharin', two homicide detectives were assigned to the investigation.

The victim: On January 23, 1983, nine-year-old Sharin' Morningstar Keenan vanished from Jean Sibelius Square. Her body turned up in a nearby rooming house nine days later.

On Tuesday, February 1, a pair of police officers called at 482 Brunswick, just north of the park. Number 482 was a rooming house, and one of the roomers reported that another tenant seemed to have skipped out — since January 24, the day after Sharin' disappeared. Who was the skipped tenant? A guy named Michael Burns who lived in the big room on the second floor.

The two officers let themselves into the Burns room. It held a single bed, an electric heater, two small tables, two chairs, a cabinet, a dresser, a hot plate and a functioning refrigerator. The room was tidy, and nothing appeared to be disturbed or suspicious. One of the officers opened the refrigerator. That was the instant when the missing person case turned irretrievably into a murder investigation. Jammed into the otherwise empty fridge was Sharin's body. As the autopsy revealed later that day, she had been raped and strangled. The search for Michael Burns got underway.

The first fact that the two homicide detectives heading the investigation learned about the man was that his name was not Michael Burns. He was Dennis Melvyn Howe, he was forty-two, and he had a criminal record for sexual and other offences dating back to 1957. Howe had served seventeen years in prison before he was paroled less than a year before the Sunday when Sharin' was murdered. The police knew plenty more about Howe: that he was stocky, five-nine and 165 pounds, that he chain-smoked unfiltered Players, had scarred ear drums and was hard of hearing, that he had a small gap between his upper front teeth, drank beer, liked country music, was left-handed, possessed a deep jovial laugh, and that he favoured the word "turkey" as a term of denigration.

It seemed that Howe also had a talent for invisibility. The cops couldn't find him, couldn't catch a clue to his whereabouts, couldn't come up with a witness who might point them in Howe's direction. A $100,000 reward for his apprehension was offered, and his story was dramatized on the TV show, *America's Most Wanted*. The money and the television program drew hundreds of tips. But none of them ever led to Howe.

Where, in all the years since Sharin's murder, was Dennis Melvyn Howe? Maybe dead. Maybe buried with other paupers in a potter's field. Or maybe

The crime scene: It was in the room circled above, at 482 Brunswick Avenue, across from Sibelius Square, that police found Sharin's murdered body.

he was sitting in a country-music bar somewhere, drinking beer, chain-smoking unfiltered Players, speaking in a loud voice to a stranger across the table, offering his opinion of Toronto cops.

"A bunch of turkeys."

GEORGINA LEIMONIS, KNOWN TO FAMILY and friends as "Vivi," was twenty-three years old, a hairdresser, bright and vivacious, and lived with her dad in the Beach neighbourhood of Toronto's east end. But when an old high-school pal named Tom Drambalas took her out on the evening of April 5, 1994, the two drove far from the Beach across the city to a smart eating spot at the corner of Davenport and Bedford in the Annex. The cafe was called Just Desserts, and Vivi had never before visited it.

As the name implies, Just Desserts specialized in pastries, gelato, exotic coffees. It became such a hot gathering place among a mostly young crowd that on many nights, the line of patrons waiting for a table stretched from the front door along Davenport and around the corner on Bedford. The delay wasn't long on the night Tom and Vivi arrived, and as it got close to eleven P.M., they were still sitting over their coffee at a table in the window.

At 10:57, four men entered the cafe. The four were black and in their twenties. They glanced around the room, exchanged looks with one another, and left. Eleven minutes later, at 11:08, three of the four men returned. The tallest of the three was carrying a double-barrelled shotgun. The three shouted at the patrons and herded Vivi, Tom and all the others to the back of the room. The tall man waved his shotgun at the crowd while his two partners stripped wallets and handbags from the patrons. One patron, Filipo Pastore, refused to give up his money. A robber, the one wearing a black toque, beat Pastore on the head. "Let's go!" the robber with the shotgun shouted. He seemed to be growing edgy at the violent byplay between his partner and Pastore. A few seconds later, the shotgun went off. The blasts from both barrels smacked into Vivi Leimonis, and she fell bleeding to the floor. The three robbers ran out the front door of the cafe, climbed into a waiting car, a white Mazda Protege driven by the fourth man, and sped away. The time was exactly eleven minutes after eleven.

The killer: Dennis Melvyn Howe, the tenant of the room at 482 Brunswick and a man with a long record of sex offences, was almost certainly Sharin's murderer, but he has evaded the police to this day.

Wanted: These men caught on video

Surveillance camera inside Just Desserts cafe shows one suspect in toque, left, one in baseball cap, right, and third man in rear.

How it happened

1 10:57 p.m.
Four men enter cafe, look around and leave.

Just Desserts

2 11:08
Three men return, one armed with a shotgun, and herd customers to the back of the cafe.

3 11:11
Robbers take customers' cash, purses and wallets and assault four people.

4 11:11
As one man is being punched, gun goes off hitting a woman sitting against

5 11:12
Suspects flee in a car heading northwest along

4 sought after woman dies in 'crash' robbery

BY JOSEPH HALL
AND HENRY STANCU
STAFF REPORTERS

It stole more than the hope and beauty of Georgia Leimonis' young life; as if that loss were not ghastly enough.

For some people in Metro it took another piece of their faith in this city.

"If you can't be safe in a place like that, where can you be safe?" said one woman yesterday outside Just Desserts, where Leimonis was murdered by a shotgun blast during what police call a "crash" robbery in the crowded cafe.

"It's getting so that you can't leave your home without fear — and it seems a lot of people aren't safe even there," the woman said as she huddled under an umbrella, wet snow falling around her feet.

An angry Metro police Chief William McCormack called it a

GEORGIA LEIMONIS: Died from two shotgun blasts.

"If you cannot sit in a restaurant and enjoy yourself without being murdered by thugs ..."

It happened just after 11 p.m. Tuesday.

Leimonis — ViVi to her large family and many friends

Davenport and Bedford Rds.

Like about 20 others in the cafe, the 23-year-old East York woman was there to converse with companions over cakes and coffee when three men burst through the door and ordered patrons and staff to the back of the room at gunpoint.

The three thieves — a fourth man waited outside in a car — began to work their way roughly through the crowd, demanding money and wallets, when things went horribly wrong.

The gunman, who according to witnesses was visibly nervous and possibly drugged, suddenly pulled the trigger of his sawed-off shotgun.

About 2 metres (7 feet) away, Leimonis took the full blast, suffering mortal wounds to the left upper chest from two simultaneous bursts. The pellets ripped into her heart and lungs, dam-

The killing of Georgina Leimonis during an armed robber at an Annex restaurant called Just Desserts on April 5, 1994, was said to have "robbed Toronto of its innocence."

Vivi had been hit by more than 200 shotgun pellets, and she died early on the day after the shooting. The police sealed off access to Just Desserts with wooden barriers and yellow crime-scene tape, but people crossed the barriers to fill the entrance with flowers and cards in mourning of Vivi. The media registered shock that such a terrible crime had taken place in the "trendy" Annex. "Nobody," one newspaper story declared, "will ever again feel safe in even the most privileged parts of Toronto."

A security camera had kept a continuous record of events at Just Desserts' front door, and it caught the four robbers on tape. The tape, released by police to local television stations, played repeatedly on newscasts. Two TV viewers, watching the tape and acting independently of one another, decided they had a story to tell. They told police they recognized a man on the Just Desserts video tape, the tall man, the one carrying the double-barrelled shotgun. His name was Lawrence Brown.

On April 14, nine days after Vivi Leimonis's death, Brown surrendered to the police. Three other men were arrested at the same time. One was Mark Jones, the alleged driver of the getaway Mazda; another was Gary Francis, who was said to be the robber in the black toque, the one who beat up Filipo Pastore; and the third was O'Neil Grant, suspected of being the final robber in the cafe. All four were committed to trial on varying charges of murder, manslaughter and armed robbery.

Both the preliminary hearing and the pre-trial motions in the case became tangled in disputes over evidence, in accusations of racism, in differences among defence lawyers, in arguments between lawyers and their clients. In the course of these proceedings, which eventually stretched over many years, a judge concluded that the evidence against Mark Jones, the alleged driver, wasn't sufficient to send him to trial. Jones walked free. The other three, who remained in custody from the day of their arrests, began their long-delayed day in court on April 28, 1999.

After a long trial, on Saturday, December 11, 1999, the jury brought in its verdicts. Lawrence Brown: guilty of murder and of twelve counts of armed robbery. Gary Francis: guilty of manslaughter, of the assault on Filipe Pastore, and of the twelve counts of armed robbery. O'Neil Grant: not guilty. Judge Trafford sentenced Brown to life in prison with no chance of parole for twenty-five years. And he gave Francis fifteen years in prison with a credit of seven years for the five and a half years he had served during the proceedings against him.

As for O'Neil Grant, of whose guilt the jury had a reasonable doubt, it was he who provoked the overhaul of Canada's Immigration Act. Grant had arrived in Toronto, an eleven-year-old Jamaican boy, in 1983, and by the time he was twenty, he had become a crack addict with a record of convictions on eighteen weapons and drug charges. The Immigration and Refugee Board ordered Grant to be deported in 1992. Grant appealed the order to the Board's appeal division where, on November 30, 1993, an adjudicator stayed the deportation. "[Grant] should be allowed to prove himself," the adjudicator ruled. Grant remained in Toronto, and four and a half months later, police arrested him for the robbery and killing at Just Desserts.

"The deportation system failed us," Sergio Marchi said in the House of Commons not long after Grant's arrest. Marchi was the Minister of Immigration, and in 1995, he guided through the Commons new legislation that made it simpler and speedier under the Immigration Act to deport immigrants convicted of a crime. The legislation's official designation was Bill C-44, but among politicians and bureaucrats in the Department of Immigration, it was known as the Just Desserts Bill, named for the chic Annex cafe that closed not long after the murder of Vivi Leimonis.

VINCENT MASSEY HAD A PLAN. He didn't want the case of his murdered cousin Bert, shot by Bert's maid, Carrie Davies, to come to trial. Too embarrassing for the Massey family, Vincent declared, nasty publicity for all the relatives, especially for Vincent himself, who was the family's effective chief and its most snobbish member. Vincent thought he knew how to avoid such a humiliation: if Carrie were declared of unsound mind, then, under existing laws, she would be committed to the insane asylum with no trial and therefore no publicity. Vincent took his plan to Ontario's Conservative Attorney-General, I.B. Lucas, who agreed to go along with the Masseys. The family breathed sighs of relief.

This was before Dr. Nelson Beemer became involved in the case. Dr. Beemer was a genial man with advanced notions about the treatment of the mentally ill, and as head of the Mimico Lunatic Asylum, he was in a position to put his notions into practice. The court sent Carrie to Beemer for an assessment, and it took the doctor only a day or two to conclude that Carrie's sanity was intact. Beemer also found himself sympathetic to Carrie's explanation of her behaviour toward her employer on the evening of February 8.

As Carrie told Beemer, it seemed that Bert, like many Toronto gentlemen of his class, enjoyed the custom of taking maids to his bed. He hadn't forced himself on Carrie yet, but she was aware of the practice because her older sister, a former maid, had warned her of it. Carrie felt certain that Bert was preparing his seduction. The night before the shooting, Bert kissed her in the kitchen, presented her with a three-dollar pearl ring, and directed her to his bedroom where he asked her to put on Mrs. Massey's underwear. When Carrie declined, Bert opened his dressing gown and pressed his exposed self against her. Carrie fled to her room. The next night, terrified of the horrors that she had no doubt her master was plotting, she armed herself with Bert's revolver, the one that young Charlie used for target practice in the basement, and waited for Bert to arrive home. Then she shot him.

With Dr. Beemer's declaration of Carrie's sanity, the trial proceeded on Friday, February 26, just eighteen days after the shooting. Hartley Dewart, a leading Toronto counsel, represented Carrie. After the crown attorney, E.A. Du Vernet, presented the prosecution's case, Dewart summoned Carrie to the witness stand. For the first time in public, guided by Dewart's questions, she told her story, the shocking tale of Bert's sexual menaces and her own terrified response.

E.A. Du Vernet was gentle with Carrie on cross-examination.

"Did you pull the trigger because you were angry with Mr. Massey?" he asked.

"No," Carrie answered in a firm voice. "I believed he would try to accomplish what he had started to do the day before."

Next morning, Saturday, Hartley Dewart addressed the jury. "Never before," he said, "has an honorable and virtuous girl been charged with the crime of murder because she successfully resisted the attacks of her master upon her person."

The twelve jurors took only a few minutes to settle on a verdict. They acquitted Carrie, a decision that the presiding judge, Chief Justice Sir William Mulock — a member of the Cawthra family, regarded in Toronto social circles as the principal rival to the Masseys — said he concurred with. Carrie walked from the courtroom a free woman.

Over the following years, much of both good and bad fortune occurred in the lives of the trial's principals. Hartley Dewart, Carrie's lawyer, was elected to the provincial legislature as a Liberal member in 1916, was named head of the Ontario Liberal Party, lost his seat in 1919, and gave up politics in favour of a return to a full-time career in the law. Charlie Massey, Bert's son, went into law himself, winning the gold medal as Osgoode Hall Law School's top student in his graduating year; then he switched to business where he climbed to the presidency of the soap conglomerate, Lever Brothers. Carrie Davies married a man named Charles Brown who made a marginal living as a market gardener, roofer and school caretaker. He and Carrie lived in the small Ontario towns of Norval and Huttonville in humble circumstances. The couple had two children, a boy and a girl, but it wasn't until many years after Carrie's death that the two learned from a journalist in the 1980s that their mother had been the Annex maid who murdered a Massey and got away with it.

❧ CHAPTER EIGHT ❧

The Literary Annex

THE BLACK DOG OF depression came on Morley Callaghan in July of 1938. He had fallen into despair over events in Europe: the gathering triumph of the fascists in the Spanish Civil War, the millions of Russians put to death by Stalin, the spread of Hitler's power in central Europe. But more personally, he was terrified that he had been deserted by the writing talent that had brought enormous acclaim over the previous decade for his novels and short stories. The immediate reason for such doubts came with the fate of his eight most recent stories. He had submitted the stories to magazines and literary journals in Europe and North America, and all eight drew rejection slips.

"I can remember," he wrote much later, "the summer night when I was out on the street at twilight, walking slowly up and down in front of my house, asking myself what was going to happen to me. I was broke. I couldn't write anything anyone wanted to read. Was I a morning glory? After all the quick early successes, was I all washed up? I felt an apprehensive chill, thinking of the new life ahead, and then a moment of blind panic bewildered me and left me in a sweat."

Callaghan had returned to Toronto, his home town, in 1936 after a couple of years with his wife, Loretto, and their small son, Michael, in Pennsylvania and New York City. He found a new home for the three of them in the second-floor apartment of the house at 456 Brunswick

Morley Callaghan, shown in a 1948 photo, was an Annex resident from 1936 to 1951, a period when he wrote some of his most memorable novels as well as some of his most forgettable books. OPPOSITE: In 1936, Morley Callaghan lived and wrote in the house on the right, 456 Brunswick, moving the following year to an apartment in the house on the left, 32 Wells, where he stayed until 1940.

From 1940 to 1951, Callaghan, his wife, two young sons and his typewriter occupied the upper flat of the house at 123 Walmer Road before he finally decamped for a grander residence in Rosedale.

Avenue, and it was here that Callaghan produced some of his most enduring work. He wrote the novel *They Shall Inherit the Earth,* put together the collection *Now That April's Here and Other Short Stories,* and he began *More Joy In Heaven,* the novel that he completed in 1937 after his second son, Barry, was born and the family moved into a larger apartment at 32 Wells Avenue, one house away and immediately around the corner from the Brunswick address.

Then came Callaghan's dark mood, the twilight walk of anxiety on the Wells Avenue sidewalk. It was a bleak moment signalling a change for Callaghan that lasted a decade, a period in which the writing of the kind of novels and short stories that his early reputation rested on took second place to other kinds of literary and non-literary work. Still living in the Wells apartment, he rewrote two plays that had been tucked in a drawer, incomplete, for two or three years. Broadway producers optioned both, but neither reached the stage in New York. One of the plays, *To Tell the Truth,* was performed in Toronto several years later, in 1948. Scholar and literary critic Northrop Frye attended the play's opening night and later noted in his diary that he found *To Tell the Truth* "most inept & fatuous."

In 1940, the Callaghan family moved two blocks east to a house at 123 Walmer Avenue, where they rented an apartment on the second floor of the fourplex and where Callaghan scouted for paying tasks even further removed from novel writing than the plays had been. World War II had begun, and Callaghan took an assignment from the Canadian Navy to write the script for a film documentary about corvettes, a job that called for a trip of several weeks to Halifax and out to sea on board one of the ships. Back in Toronto, in 1943, CBC Radio hired him to appear on a weekly thirty-minute talk show called *Of Things to Come.* Conversation on the show ranged over a variety of topics, many of them related to war themes, and for two periods, the program went on the road from its Toronto studio, sending Callaghan on a series of town hall broadcasts across the country.

Callaghan was a man with a gift of the gab who kept himself informed on many subjects beyond the world of literature (and held strong opinions even on matters he knew little about). These qualities made him a natural for such a forum as *Of Things to Come,* and in the years that followed, he became a regular panellist or host on similar radio programs including *Citizen's Forum* (the successor to *Of Things to Come*), *Beat the Champs,* and *Now I Ask You.* Some of the shows featured quiz elements, but they relied mostly on bright and articulate talk that appealed to the CBC audience. This kind of work peaked for Callaghan with *Fighting Words,* the weekly television program of the 1950s and 1960s that was chaired by drama critic Nathan Cohen and also included as a panellist psychologist William Blatz. The show was given to argumentative discussion of lively issues, and it elevated Callaghan to a status as a national celebrity among viewers who may have been only vaguely aware that he was also the author of some of the country's most accomplished novels.

Dennis Lee, shown here at a 1976 poetry reading, lived at 474 Brunswick Avenue when he composed the poems that won him a 1974 Governor General's Award.

The fiction that Callaghan wrote during his years at 123 Walmer represented a fallow period. One was a novel for teenage boys titled *Luke Baldwin's Vow,* and another novel, *The Varsity Story,* was tied to a fund-raising campaign by his alma mater, the University of Toronto. But late in the 1940s, he began writing a novel that belonged in the tradition of his books of the 1930s. This was *The Loved and the Lost,* and it would win the Governor General's Award for Fiction in 1951. That was also the year when Callaghan moved from the Annex to a home he bought on Dale Avenue in Rosedale. It was there that his career prospered on two levels, as a writer of novels that received admiring reviews and as a sought-after commentator on local and world issues. Callaghan lived in the Dale house until his death in 1990.

"EVERYBODY LIVES ON BRUNSWICK AVENUE sooner or later," the novelist Katherine Govier wrote in the first sentence of her short story "Brunswick Avenue." Govier knew what she was talking about since she lived at three addresses on the street, number 411, next door at 409 and across the road at 398, in the years between 1971 and 1977 when she was at the beginning of a productive career in fiction.

And it was true; Govier was hardly alone as a Brunswick novelist, poet or editor in those years. Marian Engel lived just down the block at number 338 while she wrote her novel *Bear*, which won the Governor General's Award in 1975. During some of the same years, Sylvia Fraser rented the ground floor apartment at 382, a sunny place with white and silver decor, where she wrote three of her novels. And Dennis Lee lived further north on the next Brunswick block, at number 474, when he composed *Civil Elegies and Other Poems*, a Governor General's Award winner in 1974.

It wasn't absolutely necessary for an Annex writer to live on Brunswick. M.T. Kelly and his family arrived on Kendal Avenue in 1984, and three years later, he won a Governor General's Award for his novel *A Dream Like Mine*. The 1970 GG winner in poetry was bpNichol for *The Cosmic Chef* and other collections of his work, written for the most part while Nichol, a member of the Therafields therapy group, shuffled between four different addresses on Admiral Road. Novelist Barbara Gowdy lived at 40 Walmer Road from 1991 to 1996, a period when she produced *Mr. Sandman*, the book that got her career on track for bigger things. And the same applied earlier to M.G. Vassanji, a resident at 35 Walmer while he wrote much of *The Gunny Sack*, which won the 1990 Commonwealth Prize for best first novel and served as a warm-up for *The Book of Secrets*, winner in 1994 of the first Giller Prize for best Canadian novel.

Gwendolyn MacEwen was a Governor General's poetry winner twice, once for *The Shadow Maker*, in 1970 before she moved into the Annex, and a second time for *Afterworlds* in 1987 after she moved out. In between, she rented the ground floor apartment in the house at 73 Albany from 1978 to 1983. It wasn't a happy period for MacEwen, who suffered from depression and difficulties with alcohol. Through the day, she kept the curtains drawn on the windows of her Albany apartment, and she liked to sit through the night in the twenty-four-hour doughnut shop at the corner of Bloor and Walmer.

Susan Cre

Gwendolyn and Milton Acorn, around 1960.

According to MacEwen's biographer, Rosemary Sullivan, the Albany neighbourhood suited MacEwen's poetic temperament. "There was a European feel to the Annex," Sullivan writes. "It was tolerant of heterogeneity [and] it felt like a downtown cross-section where several worlds met." MacEwen didn't venture far when she left Albany, shifting quarters just a few blocks east and slightly south to 240 Robert Street where she made her home until she died, alone and just forty-six, on November 30, 1987. A few years later, the small and nameless park at the Walmer traffic circle a block north of MacEwen's favourite all-night doughnut shop became officially the Gwendolyn MacEwen Park.

FOR MACEWEN AND FOR writers of every sort — novelists, poets, journalists, authors of biographies and other works of nonfiction — the Annex has been a welcoming home during much of its existence. This was particularly true in the decades following the Second World War, the reason largely being that, along with the Bohemian atmosphere that writers such as MacEwen found congenial, the Annex price was right Rooms and small flats in the neighbourhood houses came at a reasonable bargain for young writers at the beginning of their careers, and for those who made successes, the purchase price of Annex real estate stuck close to the affordable level. That balance has dramatically tilted in recent years; while many writers on the prosperous end of the scale, mostly those in journalism and other nonfiction forms, have continued to make the Annex their neighbourhood of choice, younger writer seeking garret accommodation have bypassed it in favour of less pricey areas of the city.

MacEwen lived, often unhappily, in the ground-floor apartment of this house at 73 Albany from 1978 to 1983.

The writing life, principally nonfiction division, of Douglas — now George — Fetherling describes the perfect Annex arc of the late twentieth century. Fetherling has written more than fifty books in every field including poetry and fiction. He grew up in West Virginia, arrived in Toronto as a teenager and Vietnam War resister in the late 1960s, and lived at seven Annex addresses from the early 1970s to the late 1990s. He started in what he later described as "an attic bachelorette" on Bernard Avenue near Avenue Road, a place that was "barely big enough to live in when the hide-a-bed was extended full length." A poet friend told him about another apartment for rent in "a big dirty old bow-windowed house" on the east side of Spadina, midway between Bloor and Dupont. Fetherling moved in but still kept the Bernard bachelorette. "So that for awhile I had two cheap little places instead of one decent one; two cheap little places but very different from each other, thus facilitating the continuance of parallel lives, the professional and the personal, the public and the private, the journalistic and the literary."

George — formerly Douglas — Fetherling, author of more than fifty books, sits on the porch of the house at 247 Albany, the last of his seven Annex addresses from the 1970s to the late 1990s.

Later, Fetherling occupied a succession of modest Annex apartments and communal houses, including a ground floor flat on Howland Avenue near "a socialist agitator who was Earle Birney's mistress." By the early 1980s, he grew sufficiently flush from his writing that he upgraded from renter class to owner category. This was the same period when he married Janet Inkstetter, an antiquarian bookseller. Inkstetter took over Annex Books, a store at Bathurst and Dupont, in 1983, two years after she and Fetherling purchased 247 Albany Avenue around the corner from the store. In the Albany quarters, Fetherling wrote at his accustomed rate of two or three books per year, a wide-ranging catalogue that included the definitive dictionary of world assassins of all periods and countries.

Fetherling's marriage to Inkstetter broke up in the late 1990s, and not long afterwards, he sold the Albany house. His first notion was "to give it to the homeless in order to make some of them homefull." Zoning restrictions and the prospect of a revolt by other Albany homeowners changed Fetherling's mind, and he sold the house at a bargain price to a neighbour with a large family. Just before the sale, Fetherling fell ill and underwent a successful operation to repair the arterial blood flow to his brain. On his recovery, he ended his Annex life in two fell swoops by changing his name to George Fetherling and moving to Vancouver.

Janet Inkstetter, a leading antiquarian bookseller, opened her store at Bathurst and Dupont in 1983.

NONFICTION WRITERS IN EARLIER Annex history tended to write as an afterthought to careers in other fields. That was true of Pelham Edgar, the longtime professor of English at Victoria College. Edgar, who lived from 1917 to 1946 in the mansion at 286 St. George Street inherited from his family, was noted as the university's trail-blazing champion of D.H. Lawrence and T.S. Eliot and as a mentor to Northrop Frye. His main contribution to letters came with his autobiography, *Across My Path,* which Frye edited, a task he found taxing ("there are five chunks of the memoir that are salvageable," Frye wrote in his diary at the beginning of the editing in June 1950). An Edgar colleague at Vic, Charles Sissons of the classics department, lived at 64 Admiral from 1920 to 1949, and during that time,

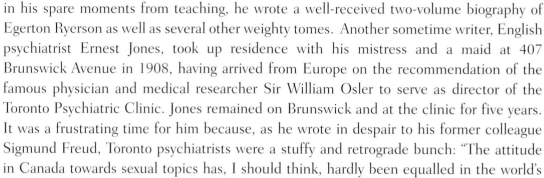

The psychiatrist Ernest Jones lived at 407 Brunswick with his mistress and his maid from 1908 to 1913 before returning to Europe where, many years later, he wrote his classic two-volume biography of Sigmund Freud.

in his spare moments from teaching, he wrote a well-received two-volume biography of Egerton Ryerson as well as several other weighty tomes. Another sometime writer, English psychiatrist Ernest Jones, took up residence with his mistress and a maid at 407 Brunswick Avenue in 1908, having arrived from Europe on the recommendation of the famous physician and medical researcher Sir William Osler to serve as director of the Toronto Psychiatric Clinic. Jones remained on Brunswick and at the clinic for five years. It was a frustrating time for him because, as he wrote in despair to his former colleague Sigmund Freud, Toronto psychiatrists were a stuffy and retrograde bunch: "The attitude in Canada towards sexual topics has, I should think, hardly been equalled in the world's history: slime, loathing and disgust are the only terms to express it." In 1913, perhaps hurried on his way by an allegation of sexual harassment that involved someone other than his mistress and his maid, Jones moved to more congenial professional surroundings in Europe where, many years later in the 1950s, he wrote the classic biography of his friend Freud.

Unlike Jones, Sissons and Edgar, B.K. Sandwell was exclusively a writer and editor. He edited *Saturday Night* magazine for nineteen years, the last nine of them, ending in 1951, while he lived in the graceful apartment building at 41 Spadina Road. Sandwell was the first of three Annex residents to hold the top job at *Saturday Night* (not to mention an *SN* assistant editor of the late 1890s, Joseph Clark, who lived on Howland Avenue; Clark was later the editor of the *Star Weekly* and the father of Gregory Clark, whose long and productive career as a journalist and author eclipsed that of the senior Clark). Robert Fulford, *Saturday Night*'s editor from 1968 to 1987, rented at 141 Albany from 1969 to 1971. That was long enough for Fulford and his wife, author and journalist Geraldine Sherman, to get burgled three times before lighting out to safer territory several blocks to the north. John Fraser, who succeeded Fulford as the magazine's editor and remained on the job

Robert Fulford, author, journalist and editor of Saturday Night *magazine from 1968 to 1987, lived in the Annex in the early 1970s just long enough to be burgled three times.*

until 1995, lived for his entire term at 104 Bernard Avenue until he moved south to Massey College when he was appointed Master of the college.

It was Fulford who, three decades after his departure from Albany Avenue, noted that "late at night [in the Annex], if you listen closely, you may pick up one dominant sound: the clicking of word-processor keys." Fulford was underlining his point that "the Annex has been the most literary section of Toronto" and that "the impression that writers sometimes outnumber houses is not always false." The most persuasive example of this truth, he decided, was the pair of adjoining Georgian houses on Howland where Sandra Martin,

Two future novelists lived twenty years apart in the same bedroom of the tiny house at 75A Spadina Road: Graeme Gibson as a boy in the 1940s and Matt Cohen as a university student in the 1960s.

the journalist, and her husband Roger Hall, the historian, lived next door to Ron Graham, the author and journalist, and his wife, Gillian MacKay, the art critic. Among the two couples, Fulford figured, they had written and edited two dozen books plus magazine and newspaper articles beyond count.

FOR DECADES, THERE WERE Margaret Atwood sightings on the Annex fringes. She got her BA at Victoria College, a block southeast of the Annex. In the summer of her graduation from Vic, 1961, she lived in a house owned by Jay Macpherson, the Victoria lecturer and poet; the house was at 15 Berryman Street in Yorkville. A couple of summers later, between the two years of her Harvard MA studies, she worked as a cashier in the coffee shop of the hotel, which later became the Venture Inn, on the non-Annex side of Avenue Road south of Davenport. In the early 1970s, she lived in a house at 27 Hilton Avenue up the Casa Loma hill from the Annex. And in the same period, when she met her companion-to-be, the novelist Graeme Gibson, the first time the couple stepped out together, they had a meal at a Japanese restaurant on the second floor of a building at Bloor and Spadina.

In 1985, Atwood crossed deep into the neighbourhood itself when she and Gibson bought a house, once occupied by Therafields people, in the east Annex. For Gibson, the Annex was already familiar territory from his younger years, when he lived with his mother and brother at 75A Spadina from 1941 to 1946. (Two decades later, the Spadina house was converted into a co-op, and one of the tenants in the mid-1960s, a student and beginning writer, was the novelist Matt Cohen, who occupied and wrote in the very room that had once been Gibson's childhood bedroom.) With the Atwood-Gibson move to the new house, there were now Atwood encounters inside the actual Annex borders, and not all of them were of a literary nature.

"Oh," neighbours said to Atwood after a few months, "you're the other woman on the street who takes a lot of taxis."

"Who's the first?" Atwood asked.

"The call girl up the block."

Atwood settled in. She became a familiar at People's Bar & Eatery, a family-run establishment near Dupont and Spadina that offered small and ancient juke boxes at all six of its booths. She attended sessions with her massage therapist in a St. George apartment building. She worked in her gardens, back and front; the one in the back included as exotic decor a gargoyle that had once served as the head piece to the swimming pool in the house next door, the first private swimming pool constructed in Toronto.

Margaret Atwood, shown here in a 1971 photograph, lived, worked and got her education at various locations on the edges of the Annex until 1985 when she and her partner, Graeme Gibson, bought a house deep in the Annex itself.

And Atwood wrote books.

This meant that the Annex could claim itself as the place of origin of novels that won prizes of an unprecedented range and number. England's Booker Prize, for example; Atwood got it in 2000 for *The Blind Assassin*. She won the Giller in 1996 for *Alias Grace*. Atwood novels took the Dashiell Hammet Prize, the Sunday Times Award for Literary Excellence, the Trillium Book Award, and enough other honours to put the Annex on the world's literary map in ways undreamed of in the time of Morley Callaghan's walk of despair sixty years earlier.

CHAPTER NINE

The Annex's Later Look

UNO PRII USED TO tell a one-sentence story on himself. Prii, who died at age seventy-seven in November 2000, was an architect who probably designed more Toronto apartment buildings than any other architect in the city's history, almost 300 of them, and the funny story about himself that he liked to repeat concerned one of his creations. It seemed that an irate tenant in a Prii apartment building called him on the telephone one day and bellowed, "When Harry K. Thaw shot Stanford White in 1906, he killed the wrong architect!"

Prii took delight in repeating the caller's one-liner. He never minded criticism, especially from tenants in the buildings that he designed, and he always added the detail that the man on the phone with the Stanford White crack lived in a Prii apartment building in the Annex. Prii designed six Annex apartment high-rises, all in the style distinctive to him, which means that, for better or worse, whether one agrees or disagrees with the complaining phone caller, Prii had as much influence as any architect, builder or developer on the post-World War II changes in the look of the Annex.

Prii was born in Estonia, the son of an architect. He studied civil engineering in Stockholm, then emigrated in 1950 to Canada, where he enrolled at the University of Toronto's School of Architecture. It annoyed Prii that the ideals that the school seemed to him to embrace at the time were those of Mies Van Der Rohe and Corbusier, the Bauhaus

The apartment building at 44 Walmer Road offers Prii's characteristic white facing and sculpted curves, but the original balcony railings that looked like children's paper cutouts were removed from the building before this photo was taken in 2001.

*The architect
Uno Prii designed a
half-dozen apartment
buildings that changed the
look of the Annex in the
1960s.*

*RIGHT: The Vincennes, a
Prii-designed apartment
house with his familiar
white facing and swooping
curve described by the line
of balconies, occupies the
site of the old Timothy
Eaton mansion.*

and Stark Modernism. Straight lines, cubist shapes. Prii rebelled against the orthodoxy. He liked circles and loops and curves in his architecture, and when he opened an office in Toronto in 1957 and attracted a clientele of apartment developers, he applied his own preferences to the buildings he designed, first to a modest degree, then in full-blown Miami Beach mode.

The Vincennes, fifteen storeys, on the site of the old Timothy Eaton mansion at Spadina and Lowther, is earlier Prii, relatively modest in its reaction to straight lines. It has all-white facing and a line at the front, described by the placing of the balconies, that drops in a long swooping curve. A near neighbour of the Vicennes is the building at 44 Walmer. It is thirteen storeys tall, predominantly white-faced and, until 2001, it was dressed in balcony railings that suggested in their design children's paper cutouts, with the emphasis on circles and whimsy, in a look that was sculpted and insouciant. When the building's new owner ordered a renovation in 2001, the first things to go were the balcony railings, an act that, if Prii were still living, would have struck him as the equivalent of painting a moustache on the Mona Lisa.

The most imposing of Prii's Annex apartment houses is on Prince Arthur close to the corner of Avenue Road. Twenty Prince Arthur is twenty-two storeys, massive, monumental and shocking. It boasts the usual Prii touches, the white facing, the glass, the curvy lines. But what most seizes the attention about the building, what becomes the first and lasting impression, are the huge flying buttresses. There are sixteen of them, eight at the front and eight at the back. They are evenly spaced, and they curve from the roof to the base, dropping imperceptibly at first and then with a jutting rush into the landscaped grounds that surround the building. Prii's idea with the flying buttresses was to combine old and new, medieval and modern. He may have succeeded, but it remains a jolt to discover flying buttresses on a non-ecclesiastical building put up in the mid-twentieth century near the corner of Bloor and Avenue Road.

MODES OF TRANSPORTATION, PARTICULARLY automobiles and subways, were what led to the major difference in the postwar look of the Annex. The automobiles belonged to people who lived in neighbourhoods to the north of the Annex and needed to get to their jobs in the city's downtown in a hurry. To accommodate them, Toronto's planners and politicians widened Spadina Road and Avenue Road by a couple of lanes each. Ancient Annex trees were uprooted to make room for the extra lanes, and the new constancy and speed of traffic led inexorably to the conversion of these two main Annex thoroughfares from predominantly residential to mostly commercial. St. George, together with Bloor, which had always taken a significant role in the city's transportation system, soon joined Spadina and Avenue Road as key streets in moving people in cars, and that development resulted in drastic alterations in those streets' makeup and look.

In this mix, the expansion of the city's subway system arrived as both good news and bad news for the Annex. First in subway growth came the extension in 1963 of the Yonge Street line in a loop up University Avenue to the St. George station at Bloor and St. George.

Then, in 1966, the east-west subway along Bloor Street opened with stops at St. George, Spadina and Bathurst. Finally, in 1978, the Spadina line went into business as an extension of the University line from the St. George station to deepest North York with stops in the Annex at two stations, one at Spadina and Bloor and another at Dupont. On the positive side, the plethora of Annex stations meant that its residents could get around the city without the bother and expense of actually owning a car. On the negative side, the arrival of the subways as an Annex fact of transportation life meant

Prii's most imposing Annex apartment building is at Twenty Prince Arthur, twenty-two storeys high with sixteen flying buttresses.

Designed by Joseph A. Medwicki in 1972, the apartment building at 190 St. George boasts a handsome Late Modern look.

that apartment buildings were bound to follow and to redraw the Annex's skyline.

Apart from a scattered handful of stray apartment houses standing isolated on subsidiary streets — one at 375 Brunswick, another at 485 Huron — the vast majority of apartment high-rises erected between the mid-1950s and the early 1970s came in clusters on the second block of Spadina Road, on lower Walmer, and all along St. George. In aesthetic terms, the buildings were a mixed bag with the tilt toward the low end in architectural beauty. Many of the apartment houses went up at a speed that left design and workmanship as an afterthought, but in the rush, a few buildings that offered visual rewards managed to rise among their more homely neighbours.

The twelve-storey, white-faced apartment house at 190 St. George emerged as one of the winners in elegant appearance. Built in 1972 and designed by Joseph A. Medwicki, the building sits at a polite remove from the street and leaves plenty of room for passers-by to observe its Late Modern good looks. It offers one relief from the tedium of most of the buildings on St. George, which is by far the Annex's busiest apartment street, and another source of comfort of a different sort comes from the building at number 169. It's a smaller apartment house, just eight storeys, designed by the firm of Crang & Boake in 1956. It undersells its charm with discreet use of glass and with balconies that are tucked at the sides.

Apartment houses on St. George such as these two aren't the only structures that rescue the street from humdrum design. The small four-storey office building at 172 St. George is one of the other rescuers; built in 1986, it represents in part a pleasant contemporary take on the Queen Anne style. At 212 St. George, a neo-Tudor mansion built in 1907 survives as a classy façade for a later assortment of low-rise living spaces. And, in 1968, the architect Barton Myers designed a four-storey office building at 240 St. George that brought together red brick, glass and recessed entrances in a smart and glossy combination. The building was commissioned by the Ontario Medical Association, but in the late 1980s, a new owner took over — the Chinese government, which converted it to use as a consulate. A decade later, followers of the exercise and meditation group Falun Gong set up a vigil on the sidewalk in front of the consulate to protest the ban on the group in China. The vigil holders, equipped with a small portable sleeping enclosure, arrived with the apparent intention of remaining deep into the future, and by the early years of the twenty-first century, Falun Gong had become a semi-permanent part of the St. George landscape.

Falun Gong demonstrators are a permanent part of the Annex landscape outside the Chinese Consulate, which occupies the building at 240 St. George originally designed by Barton Myers in 1968 as offices for the Ontario Medical Association.

The townhouses built in 2001 on the site of the old Salvation Army offices on Brunswick Avenue suggest fleetingly an update of an ancient French chateau look.

Low-rise housing showed up in modest and scattered numbers to rival the high-rise apartment buildings that dominated the post-World War II Annex. In one significant instance, a planned apartment tower was compelled to give way to living space much less gaudy and much closer to the ground. This minor miracle of neighbourhood action took place at what became the Huron-Madison Project at 25 Madison Avenue. A developer had a high-rise apartment building in the works for the site, but the Annex Residents Association and the people who lived in the on-site houses that were scheduled for demolition joined together to press for another style of housing. The result, in 1981, was a four-storey infill development that made use of the original houses and created a dozen separate units that are operated by City Housing. Huron-Madison may not be the last word in gorgeous architecture, but it is ingenious, economical and more appealing than the alternative of another tedious apartment high-rise.

The Huron-Madison Project at 25 Madison Avenue, a four-storey infill development built in 1981, was the community's answer to a developer who planned a high-rise on the site.

IF CONTEMPORARY ARCHITECTURE HASN'T added much that is memorable to the Annex's look, the Toronto Transit Commission made a contribution to the neighbourhood's optics that is a pleasure, a surprise and a secret.

The story begins with the construction of the north-south Spadina subway line in 1978. The station at Spadina had two entrances, one at the main section of the station on Spadina Road just above Bloor and the other a long block north at Kendal Avenue. Such a small number of people pass through the doors of the Kendal entrance that the ticket booth sits permanently empty of an employee. But for the few passengers arriving and leaving by way of Kendal, the TTC provided two sets of stairs, one on the east side of Spadina and the other on the west side. The west stairs lead conventionally to the street,

Instead of demolishing this 1899 Queen Anne house on Spadina Road, the TTC converted it to an entrance to the Kendal Avenue stop on the Spadina subway line.

but under the original plans, the east stairs presented a different choice in construction. Immediately over the projected exit, above ground, stood a lovely Queen Anne house designed in 1899 by Robert M. Ogilvie. The TTC's decision was to demolish the house, but, pre-demolition, the Toronto Historical Board got vigorously into the act and suggested, as an alternative, that the transit people incorporate the structure into the Kendal station. The Board persisted with its case until the TTC, admitting the artistic merit in the idea, concluded that it also worked in financial terms. In due course, the design firm Adamson Associates provided the architectural expertise, and the happy outcome is that a remodelled Queen Anne house survives as an Annex subway stop.

But the episode of architectural preservation is only the opening chapter to the story that continues with the decision of the TTC to commission a series of works by Toronto artists to spruce up many of its subway stations. Under the program, which proceeded through the late 1970s and early 1980s, Gordon Rayner enlivened the St. Clair West Station with an

The Kendal Avenue end of the TTC's Spadina subway station is home to two large pieces of art. One is this Joyce Wieland quilt that features prancing deer.

arrangement of bands of eloquent colour, Charlie Pachter contributed hockey figures to the College Street Station (handy to Maple Leaf Gardens, then home to the Maple Leafs hockey team), and other artists similarly dressed up other stations with their art. Of all the stations that blossomed in paintings and decorative works, it was the under-used Kendal stop that got the best of the deal. Astonishingly, Kendal became home to two pieces of large and joyous art. The first, on the wall at the turn in the stairs under the Queen Anne house, is by Louis de Niverville, who painted a charming rendition of a sedate rush for a train. And the second, further down the stairs and against the broad wall beyond the turnstiles, is an enormous Joyce Wieland quilt featuring prancing deer. The two works, superior pieces by significant Canadian artists, add up to a mini art gallery tucked into the corners of perhaps the most obscure subway station in all of Toronto.

CHAPTER TEN

The Spadina Expressway

THE CONCEPT OF THE road known with dread in the Annex as the Spadina Expressway was kicking around as early as 1943. City of Toronto planners had by then caught the fever for expressways from larger American cities and envisioned the Toronto of the future as a criss-cross of multi-laned highways piercing into the central city from suburbs that as yet barely existed. The scheme became refined in the next two decades. After 1953, planners and politicians spoke for a broader entity called the Municipality of Metropolitan Toronto following the legislating of the system of municipal government that merged the old city and the new suburbs. These planners and politicians particularly favoured an expressway that would loop south from Wilson Heights Boulevard in the northwest corner of North York and join near Spadina Road with the Crosstown Expressway, which would pass through the Annex just north of Bloor Street. More refinements followed. The Crosstown Expressway was dropped. The Spadina Expressway, named the William R. Allen Expressway in 1969 in honour of a former Metro Toronto chairman, was constructed as far south as Lawrence Avenue. And the intent was that it would be extended at its full length to a point close to College Street. This was a route that, of dire significance to Annex residents, would include southbound lanes down a line along Spadina Road and northbound lanes a block east at Madison Avenue.

At this early 1990s reunion of the anti-Spadina Expressway group, author Jane Jacobs is front and centre (front row, fourth from left). Others include city politicians of the pre-Spadina and post-Spadina periods: Mayor June Rowlands (front row, far left), Bill Kilbourn and Colin Vaughan (front, fourth and fifth from right) and Karl Jaffrey (second row, second from right).

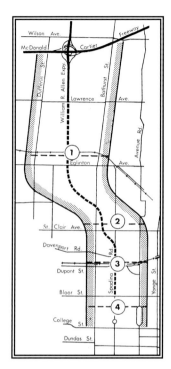

In 1970, Metro Toronto politicians and planners envisioned a criss-cross of expressways carrying traffic in and over the city.

The Annex Ratepayers Association greeted the plan with suggestions of compromise. How about, the ARA ventured, hiding the expressway underground from Dupont southward? The Metro people gave the back of their hand to such a wimpy notion and, certain they had the advantage, prepared to push the expressway to its final downtown destination. By now — the summer of 1969 — the ARA and the allies it found among eleven other ratepayers' associations representing such communities under similar siege as Forest Hill and Kensington Market had stopped making conciliatory noises. The anti-Spadina crowd came together for combat.

A paperback book, *The Bad Trip,* presented a cogent marshalling of the arguments against the expressway. It was written by the Nowlans of Admiral Road, David, who was an economist at the University of Toronto with an expertise in transportation issues, and his wife, Nadine, a social worker who later won election to city council. Their book listed the disasters that would be visited on the Annex: traffic dumped on its streets from expressway off-ramps, the racket and pollution of cars, the tearing down of Richardsonian-Romanesque houses, a sundering of the Annex into two sections on either side of the expressway. It seemed a listing of the obvious, but the book was persuasive with its confirming statistics and analysis.

Jane Jacobs brought further legitimacy to the anti-expressway cause. She was a New Yorker, a leading thinker about cities and their health and the author of a seminal book on the subject, *The Life and Death of American Cities.* In 1967, she and her family moved to Toronto and soon bought a gracious house with a generous front porch at 69 Albany Avenue.

"In the mind's eye," Jacobs wrote of the expressway's threat, "one could see the great trees and the jolly Edwardian porches falling before the onslaught."

The presence of all of the heavy hitters in the anti-Spadina cause still couldn't dissuade the politicians and bureaucrats of Metro Toronto from granting the necessary go-aheads for the expressway project — until, in the summer of 1970, just one legal hurdle remained to be cleared. This was approval from a provincial body, the Ontario Municipal Board, and that summer, in the crunch and in desperation, the anti-expressway movement retained the eminent lawyer John J. Robinette to argue its side at the OMB hearings.

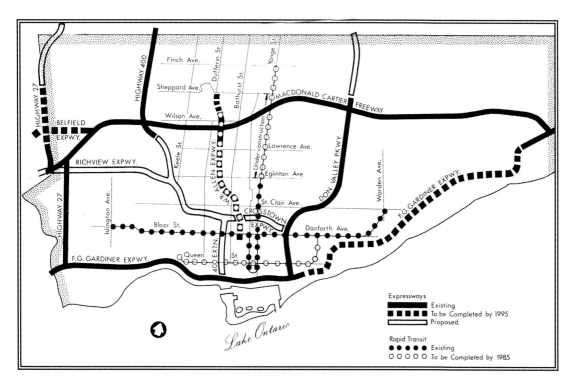

The William R. Allen Expressway, know by its friends and foes as the Spadina Expressway, was scheduled by Metro Toronto to run nonstop from north of Highway 401 to a point north of College Street in midtown Toronto.

JOHN JOSIAH ROBINETTE WAS born in 1906, the second of five children of Thomas Cowper and Edith May Robinette of 60 Spadina Road. T.C. enjoyed a reputation as the city's top criminal lawyer, the defence counsel in Toronto's bloodiest murder cases. He bought the house at 60 Spadina from Timothy Eaton's daughter and son-in-law, Margaret and Charles Burden. It was red brick, three storeys with six bedrooms on the upper floors and a den on the first floor where T.C. received his criminal clients in the evenings. John played in the Annex's backyards and streets, attended UTS a block away on Bloor Street, went with his siblings to services at Trinity Methodist Church three times each Sunday (his mother was deeply religious), and lived at 60 Spadina until his marriage in 1930 to Lois Walker, who grew up around the corner at 33 Howland Avenue. The Spadina house remained home to Edith May Robinette, T.C. having died in 1920 of a sudden stroke, until 1942

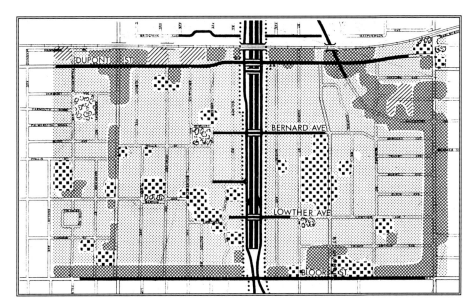

From Dupont to Bloor, in the heart of the Annex, the Spadina Expressway was routed through a principally residential neighbourhood.

when she sold it to Les Soeurs Missionnaires de Christ-Roi, a Catholic order that kept the house until a 1954 sale to a developer who put up a tall and ordinary apartment building.

When the anti-expressway people hired John Robinette, they were unaware of his early history in the Annex and his continuing affection for the area. All they knew about Robinette, which was quite enough, was that he was arguably the most accomplished courtroom lawyer in Toronto, if not Canada, equally at home with criminal and civil cases, both at trial and on appeal. For Robinette's clients in the expressway matter, it was an unexpected bonus that he, like Jane Jacobs, was horrified by the prospect of the destruction of the Annex's wonderful old houses. The difference between Jacobs and Robinette was that he had grown up with the houses.

ONE NIGHT IN 1970 when David Nowlan was attending a meeting at Toronto City Hall during the course of the expressway fight, he discovered a document that someone had placed in a spot where Nowlan was sure to come across it. The document, titled "1995 Travel Demand Study," had been recently prepared by a firm named Kates, Peat, Marwick & Company that was consulting to Metro. The report's thrust, Nowlan learned as he flipped through its pages, was that no matter how many expressways Toronto built, its traffic would be even more congested by 1995. It seemed that an anonymous whistle-blower, undoubtedly a city employee who shared the anti-Spadina sentiments, had directed to Nowlan the Kates, Peat report, which Metro Toronto would otherwise have allowed to remain unrevealed to the expressway's opponents.

Mr. or Ms Anon similarly slipped to the anti-Spadina team a paper that Alan Voorhees had presented two years earlier, in 1968, to a conference of the Town Planning Institute of England. Voorhees was a Washington, D.C., traffic planner, a respected authority in the field and a man who generally took a pro-expressway stand. The latter bias explained why Metro Toronto had hired him to appear before the OMB as a witness on Metro's behalf. But in the 1968 paper, Voorhees went in the opposite direction, celebrating rapid transit over expressways. Since Voorhees had prepared hundreds of papers over the course of his career, the anti-Spadina group would have been unlikely to discover the particular document that countered the customary Voorhees view without the intervention of the secret benefactor.

John Robinette tucked away the two documents for future reference, and on January 4, 1971, he began the sixteen-day hearing on the expressway before the OMB. The board was comprised of three men, the chair, J. A. Kennedy, and two junior members named Shrub and McGuire. Kennedy was the key, a sound lawyer (a member of the same Osgoode Hall Law School class as Robinette) and a veteran of the OMB. He was a no-nonsense chair who ran the board in the manner of a judge in court, formally and according to legal principles. Robinette was happy to play the hearing in the style that appealed to Kennedy, and even though there were no legal points to raise, Robinette handled his cross-examinations of Metro's seven witnesses — four Metro senior civil servants, a traffic engineer in private practice, another traffic engineer employed by the Toronto Transit Commission, plus Alan Voorhees, the paid expert witness from Washington — as if he were involved in courtroom litigation.

Kids Rule: today a future generation of Annex residents gets an airing en masse, less than a block away from where the expressway would have cut through the neighbourhood.

So it was that when Voorhees took the stand and sang the praises of expressways over rapid transit as the solution to traffic planning in urban centres, Robinette read to Voorhees on cross-examination Voorhees' opinions from the 1968 paper. "It appears that in our large cities," Robinette quoted, "it is very difficult to reduce congestion in the highway field by providing new facilities." Robinette repeated at length Voorhees' other 1968 views. "A motorway system can take care of our basic transportation but not necessarily our peak needs." When he had finished quoting from the paper, Robinette asked Voorhees, gently as was his custom, which side was he advocating? Expressways or subways? Voorhees waffled. Well, on the one hand, he said, expressways were preferable, but on the other hand, perhaps subways might do a better job in certain circumstances. Robinette asked Voorhees where he was headed next in his capacity as a consultant on traffic problems. Bulgaria, Voorhees said, where he was advising the government on its transportation system. Ah, wondered Robinette, what sort of system? "Rapid transit," Voorhees answered. When he stepped from the stand, Voorhees had come across as an expert who could be bought.

Sam Cass testified. He was Metro Toronto's Commissioner of Roads and Traffic, and he too championed the virtues of expressways. In Robinette's cross-examination, he brought up the Kates, Peat report, pointing out to Cass the report's conclusion: "Commensurate with this high utilization is an expected overall reduction in the level of services on the road system. The average travel speed on the road network in 1995 is expected to be 12 miles per hour and the average trip 56 minutes, as compared to 17 miles per hour and 29 minutes in 1964." Robinette asked Cass if he was familiar with the study and its conclusion.

"This is the first time I have seen it," Cass said, an answer that caused many jaws to drop in the hearing room.

Robinette later asked another Metro witness about the Kates, Peat report. The witness was Wojciech Wronski, Metro Toronto's Commissioner of Planning, and he allowed that he was aware of the report but hadn't read it because ever since it reached his office in March 1970, his staff had been busy analyzing it.

The message that Robinette's cross-examinations delivered was that maybe none of these experts and officials knew what they were talking about. This was a major part of the theme that he pursued in his final argument to the board. Metro's witnesses had not established a demand for the expressway, and to allocate millions of dollars to build one would be bad finance as well as bad planning. Perhaps a rapid transit line was the real answer, but in any event, Robinette argued, all that had emerged from the hearings was that an expressway would lead to the disruption of much of Toronto's inner city without proven benefit to the suburban automobile commuters.

J. A. Kennedy bought the Robinette argument. At the end of the hearings, he wrote a judgment indicating that he had appreciated Robinette's victories on cross-examination. He referred to "the somewhat unusual matter" of the Cass and Wronski reactions to the Kates, Peat report, and he thought the Voorhees testimony demonstrated that much more investigation was needed into the dilemma of expressways versus rapid transit. Kennedy's conclusion was that approval of the Spadina Expressway should be withheld until "a proper study has been made of the comparative cost of expressways and public transit, as well as a study of measures that can be introduced to increase transit use by limiting access to downtown by automobile, and a study to show specifically the amount of automobile traffic to downtown that can be eliminated by increasing use of public transit." The opinion that Kennedy wrote supported the anti-Spadina argument in almost all particulars.

But his judgment, strong as it was in language and reasoning, counted as just a single

The lawyer John Robinette, shown contemplating his own sculpted likeness in a ceremony at Osgoode Hall, emerged as the hearing-room hero of the Stop Spadina movement.

OMB vote. Shrub and McGuire had the other votes, and the anti-Spadina group had uneasy feelings about the two men. They were the pair who ate lunch together every day of the hearings, just the two of them without Kennedy. The lunches proved to be a bad omen. Compared to Kennedy, Shrub and McGuire wrote relatively more superficial judgments. And the judgments were in accord with one another in skating past the points Robinette had raised and in waving off the anti-expressway reaction. "In coming to a final conclusion," Shrub wrote, "it is necessary to brush aside some of the human and emotional factors which governed the position taken by a large body of the opposition." Shrub and McGuire recommended the completion of the expressway from Lawrence to College Street, and the OMB thus approved Spadina by a two-to-one vote.

BUT ALL WAS NOT FINISHED for the anti-Spadina side. Legislation permitted an appeal of the OMB decision to the Ontario cabinet; in this case, that meant the Progressive Conservative cabinet of Bill Davis, who was named his provincial party's leader and the province's premier in succession to the retired John Robarts a couple of months after the OMB ruling. With nothing to lose, the expressway's opponents filed the necessary appeal papers. These included two principal documents. One was J. A. Kennedy's dissenting judgment; it had been far more powerful than the majority judgments of Shrub and McGuire which Robinette characterized as "feeble." And the other document was a brief written by Robinette himself, the lawyer who had emerged, in the eyes of the anti-Spadina activisits, as the hero of the OMB hearings.

Bill Davis and his ministers took their time in announcing a decision, and the spring of 1971 dragged by with no word on Spadina. Davis represented a riding in Brampton where he lived northwest of Toronto, and he might be expected to prefer the expressway on which he and his constituents could theoretically speed to the big city's centre. On the other hand, Davis might decide to give his new leadership a distinctive and largely unexpected tone by going along with the radical likes of the Nowlans and Jane Jacobs.

The suspense ended on June 3 when Davis rose in the Legislature at Queen's Park and announced that he and his government had made up their minds. Davis said the process in arriving at the decision had been "agonizing." Later, it was revealed that what he was talking about was a divisive split in the cabinet over the expressway. The ministers who opposed Spadina argued that killing the expressway made both political and cultural sense. In the most recent provincial election in 1967, thirty of the ridings were decided by pluralities of fewer than 1,000 votes. Surely, the argument went, this indicated that voters wanted something new and different in government, something that an anti-expressway decision would embody. "Government," one analyst wrote, "must now reflect life styles, intangibles that are usually sloughed off." Three weeks earlier, Davis had made a decision that indicated he rec-

"Café culture" in the Annex: coffee and other stimulants of spring on Bathurst Street.

ognized such factors when he banned commercial logging in Quetico Provincial Park. In that instance, Davis chose the protection of 1,750 square miles of wilderness in Quetico over the harvesting of trees for lumber, "life styles" over commerce.

He made a similar choice on Spadina. To the joy of the anti-expressway crowd, Davis said in the legislature that he and his cabinet were ending construction of the Allen Expressway. Four years later, in 1975, he would take the edge off the decision by approving an extension of the expressway south to Eglinton Avenue. But for now, until the early twenty-first century and perhaps far beyond, the Annex and its Richardsonian-Romanesque houses were rescued from traffic and destruction.

CHAPTER ELEVEN

The Annex's Favourite Hangouts

FANNY CHADWICK WAS BORN on January 10, 1873, which meant she wasn't yet in her teens in 1884 when her father Edward moved his wife, Maria, their oldest daughter, Fanny, and her siblings into the enormous new redbrick home at 111 Howland Avenue. The house was the first built on Howland in the block north of Barton and lay directly across the street from the designated site of the Cathedral of St. Alban the Martyr. Edward Chadwick earned his excellent living as a senior partner with the law firm of Beatty, Chadwick, Blackstock & Galt on Wellington Street. He was a devout man of the Anglican faith who attended services at St. Alban's as soon as it was sufficiently constructed to receive a congregation. Mr. Chadwick's bouts of gout kept him at home on the occasional Sunday, but he took a prominent role in the church's administrative affairs and served as its treasurer for exactly twenty years. Fanny, like the other Chadwick daughters, sang in St. Alban's choir, her term lasting eleven years. But quick and impish Fanny wasn't particularly pious, and more than any activity, she was devoted to writing, As she confided to her diary, she thought of herself as a playwright, mostly of comedies, and she lived up to her own billing by completing several plays for which she additionally functioned as the producer, director and star performer.

She also provided the venue for the productions of her plays — or, more accurately,

These dancers at the annual Annex Fair in 1976 are wearing costumes of the period which also happen to be their own regular clothes.

In 1884, Edward Chadwick moved his family into the house at 111 Howland Avenue where daughter Fanny used the living room as the venue for the production of plays she wrote, directed and starred in.

her father did — since most of them were staged in the spacious Chadwick living room for enthusiastic audiences of family, friends and friends of friends. Members of the working press often attended too. On Friday evening, June 10, 1892, Fanny presented her play *Scandal,* which she advertised as "A Farce in Two Acts." A critic from the *Sunday World* showed up at the Chadwick house and pronounced the play "good and witty." *Saturday Night* magazine didn't send a reporter to cover the event, but it had impeccable sources inside the Chadwick soiree. "Miss Chadwick of Howland Avenue gave a most enjoyable theatrical evening," *Saturday Night* reported the night after the play. "Scandal, said to be exceedingly clever, was performed. The evening was brought to a close by dancing."

Fanny was prolific in her output for several years, but the number of plays she wrote fell off sharply after June 13, 1898. That was the day when she married a young lawyer named James Grayson Smith and moved into the couple's new home across town on Ontario Street. Two years later, in 1900, Fanny gave birth to a son she and James named Hugh. On January 13, 1905, two days after her thirty-second birthday, suddenly and from a cause that history has not recorded, Fanny died. Her grief-stricken father donated to St. Alban's a stained-glass window in Fanny's memory. Fanny would probably have regarded the window as too grand for her taste since it showed St. Margaret of Scotland, wife of Malcolm III, King of Scotland from 1054 to 1093. Margaret, whose principal connection to Fanny was that both women had fathers named Edward, was canonized in 1251 largely for her work in rebuilding the monastery of Iona. After Edward Chadwick's death on December 15, 1921, his family presented St. Alban's with a second stained-glass window that was positioned immediately to the left of Fanny's. The two windows are linked at the top by the ancient Chadwick motto that also appears to this day on a stained-glass window in the front hall of the former Chadwick house across the street on Howland: "In candore decus / Toujours pret," which translates as "There is honour in purity / Ever prepared."

IN WELL-TO-DO TORONTO circles of the late nineteenth century, the Annex included, most entertainments and social events were of a domestic sort, taking place in the downstairs rooms of the fine large homes. This practice was formalized in the custom of designating "receiving days" for the ladies of society, a different day of the week for each of the city's prosperous neighbourhoods. For those who lived north of Bloor, the receiving day was Friday — every other Friday — and on that day, the ladies of the Annex readied themselves and their houses to welcome guests. If an Annex hostess was unable to observe the tradition, her obligation was to place a notice in the morning newspaper: "Mrs. X will not receive this Friday or again this season."

For Annex residents who were keen to get out of the house, the choice of diversions in the immediate neighbourhood was limited. A ride on the trams of the Belt Line was an inexpensive treat, especially in warm weather when the tram doors were left open; the trip took passengers down Spadina, east on King, north on Sherbourne and west on Bloor, all for five cents, six tickets for a quarter. In the summer, the Ben Greet Players performed open-air Shakespeare on the front campus at the nearby University of Toronto. St. George Street, in season, was popular for those who liked to dress in their best gowns and suits for a promenade. And on Sundays after church, many Annex residents imitated the practice of Timothy Eaton by sitting on the front porches of their houses and offering greetings to passing friends and neighbours.

But for the most part, the chance of finding a diversion in the Annex — a meal in a good restaurant, a cocktail in a bar, a performance in a theatre devoted to plays or films — was nonexistent

Edward Chadwick and his playwright daughter Fanny are remembered in these stained-glass windows (Edward on the left, Fanny on the right) on the north wall of St. Alban's Church where Edward served for treasurer for twenty years and where Fanny sang in the choir for a dozen years.

Shown here pre-World War II, the Park Plaza Hotel (now the Park Hyatt) has reigned in elegance at the northwest corner of Bloor and Avenue Road since its construction in the late 1920s.

until deep into the twentieth century. The decision of the early developers to restrict the Annex's interior to strictly residential purposes meant that businesses devoted to the hospitality arts were confined to the main streets that bounded the Annex, principally Bloor. And even these were slow to develop. For decades, nobody in the Annex sought out establishments in their own neighbourhood for dining, drinking and entertaining, and few people from other Toronto neighbourhoods who were looking for a good time on the town made the Annex their destination of choice.

FROM THREE O'CLOCK TO six in the afternoon of May 12, 2000, the Park Hyatt Hotel, formerly the Park Plaza, threw a party in the Roof Lounge on the eighteenth floor in honour of Harold Kochberg. It was a party that put Kochberg in an unaccustomed position. His usual role was to serve drinks to patrons, not to join them in a drink himself. On this May 2000 afternoon, Harold Kochberg, known to decades of Roof drinkers as simply "Harold," the affable but discreet waiter, was celebrating his fiftieth year of bringing the patrons their cocktails and highballs. It was Harold who played a featured role over his half-century on the Roof in making it the favourite drinking spot for, among other groups, cliques and guests, Toronto's literary set.

The hotel, at the northwest corner of Bloor and Avenue Road, was built in the late 1920s on the site of the Albert Nordheimer mansion. Its construction took a protracted span of years, from 1926 to 1929, mostly because of the Taddle Creek effect. Water from the Taddle caused the building to tilt and sink and the elevators to stall, until, after long periods of experimental adjusting, a system by which the ground was perma-frozen straightened and stabilized the structure. In appearance, the Park Plaza featured a narrow arcade on the Avenue Road side, dramatic two-storey windows atop the arcade level, and, above them, solid rows of conventionally sized and closely spaced windows which gave the building a look of being perpetually up-to-date. On the very top, the hotel offered the climactic details of a small dining room, a patio with a spectacularly uninterrupted view to the south, and the smart little bar where, in May 1950, Harold Kochberg arrived for his first day of work.

Harold grew up at 22 Brunswick Avenue a few doors north of College Street and across from the YMHA. When he was ten years old, in what he describes as an alternative to getting into delinquent trouble, Harold joined the Y and took up handball. It was a game he continued to play four or five times a week for decades, first on Brunswick, then at the Y's later location in larger quarters at the southwest corner of Bloor and Spadina. He married, raised three children, bought a home in North York, kept fit on the handball court, and perfected the art of serving a drink on the Roof of the Park Plaza.

Affable but discreet, Harold Kochberg served drinks in the smart Roof Bar of the Park Plaza Hotel from 1950 to 2002.

LUNCHEON MENU

Individual Onion Soup au Gratin .50

Malpeque Oysters in Shell 1.25   Imported Skinless Sardines   1.00
Smoked Gaspe Salmon   1.10   Shrimp Cocktail   1.10
Prosciutto with Melon   .90   Marinated Herring   .75
Grapefruit Supreme   .40   Celery Olives & Radishes   .50

Curried Jumbo Shrimps
or
Poached Halibut Bonne Femme
Salad Bowl
Rolls & Butter - Tea or Coffee
1.50

TABLE D'HOTE

Fish Chowder   Fruit or Vegetable Juice   Consomme Andalouse
      Cold Vichyssoise   Jellied Consomme

Plain or Fines Herbes Omelet   1.75
Filet of Pickerel Saute Meuniere   1.85
Poached Salmon, Sauce Creme   2.00
Chicken Pot Pie Park Plaza   2.15
Veal Saute Marengo   2.25
Sirloin Cut Minute Steak Maitre D'Hotel   3.25

   Kernel Corn a la Creme   Buttered Green Peas
   Parsley Potatoes   Home Fried Potatoes

Apple Pie with Cheese   Assorted French Pastries   Vacherin Glace
Bavarian Cream, Strawberry Sce.   Assorted Ice Cream or Sherbert
   Assorted Fruit Tarts   Cantaloup or Spanish Melon
               Cheese & Crackers

      Tea   Coffee   Milk

A LA CARTE

Fancy Fruit Salad - Cottage Cheese   1.95
Shrimp Salad in Sea Shell   2.25
Cold Half Lobster en Bellevue   2.25
Cold Sliced Beef, Ham & Turkey with Italian Salami 2.10

Friday November 22nd, 1957

Sirloin steak for $3.25 was the most expensive choice for lunch in 1957 in the small dining room on the roof of the Park Plaza.

He served Ned Pratt, the renowned poet, member of the English department at nearby Victoria College, and the man whom Harold remembers as his most loquacious patron. Pratt's colleague, Northrop Frye, always accompanied by his wife, Helen, was the most low-key and soft-spoken. Frye noted in his diary that in the late afternoon of April 1, 1952, after a frustrating afternoon of lecturing on the subject of Christianity and Culture to Presbyterian ministers whom Frye found to be "philistines," he went straight to the Roof "where I met Helen and sank a couple of martinis."

The young English teachers of Ryerson College had a regular table on the Roof in the 1960s. Their number included Graeme Gibson, who later wrote dense and thoughtful novels, and Eric Wright, who, also later, made a reputation as one of Canada's leading authors of crime novels. The editors of *Maclean's* magazine formed another group of regulars, and so did the much smaller staff of *TIME* magazine's Canadian edition. One spring afternoon in 1964, the *Maclean's* people brought as their guest Edmund Wilson, the great American cultural critic who was in Toronto on an assignment for *The New Yorker*. Serrell Hillman, head of the Toronto TIME bureau, became so excited when he spotted Wilson that he bolted across the room and, inadvertently transposing his verbs, blurted to Wilson, "I've written everything you've ever read!"

The phone in the small lobby outside the Roof Bar took a beating from the patrons. Harry Bruce, *Maclean's* writer and editor of the early 1960s, was once in the act of calling his wife to say he was headed for home when his drinking companion, the brilliant and erratic cartoonist Duncan Macpherson, loomed over him. "You're not leaving, Harry," Macpherson said, and proceeded to rip the phone from the wall. That performance was perhaps topped a few years later by Eric Nesterenko, NHL hockey player of the 1950s and 1960s and the author of a *Maclean's* article about his life in the game. A fellow drinker at Nesterenko's table announced his need to use the telephone. Nesterenko excused himself and returned a few minutes later carrying the

Roof's lobby phone, which, like Macpherson, he had yanked out of the wall.

In the early 1980s, *Toronto Sun* cartoonist Andy Donato contributed a series of twenty or more caricatures of prominent Roof drinkers, almost all of them from the Canadian writing community. The caricatures have remained on display on the walls in the bar: Peter Gzowski, Mordecai Richler, June Callwood, Adrienne Clarkson (in her novelist and CBC-TV hostess mode, not in her vice-regal Governor General role). Harold Kochberg was in the habit of making a small joke about the people in the drawings.

"I spilled drinks on all of them," he liked to say.

The line was more than an exaggeration: Harold never lost a drop from a single cocktail he ever served on the Roof.

Once a Bible College, the building at 16 Spadina Road is now the Native Canadian Centre.

Built in the 1920s as the Madison, the theatre has been renamed several times, emerging first as the Midtown, then the Capri and the Eden before it finally became the Bloor.

FROM THE 1930s ONWARD, the restaurants on the north side of Bloor west of Avenue Road gave the block a lunching and dining identity. Its reputation wasn't for fine cuisine. Very few restaurants in the city could make such a claim, but the Bloor eating spots were at least distinctive in their gentility. Murray's Restaurant on the ground floor of the Park Plaza was known for its reliably bland food (rice pudding was a dessert specialty), and for its prompt and cheery service by waitresses known collectively as Miss Murray. Dinah Sweets, slightly more daring in its dishes, was one of the first restaurants to introduce adjectives to its menu ("Wonderful Chicken A La King"). The lunch counter at Palmer's Drug Store acquired fame for its egg salad sandwiches on white bread. And the Chez Paree, though its food was more Anglo-Saxon than Parisian, offered a modest chic and, in the evenings, polite jazz from a trio whose music never rose above a murmur.

The stretch of Bloor further west, from Spadina to Bathurst, was slow to acquire a personality and consisted mainly of a disparate collection of neighbourhood merchants whose stores and restaurants were fitted into the ground floors of the street's original houses. By the early 1950s, however, this part of Bloor began a transformation that made it for three decades the commercial centre for Toronto's Hungarian community. At the height of the street's Hungarian period, it was home to more than fifty merchants who had emigrated from Hungary and were carrying on business in old country products plus another couple of dozen Hungarian restaurants and other entrepreneurs advertising a vast range of special services. This was a collection that included the street's unofficial mayor, a versatile man named Dr. Z. Baranyi who presented his services at 475 Bloor West as a notary public, stamp dealer and driving instructor.

Unlike Torontonians of Chinese descent with their various Chinatowns and the Italians with their Little Italy, Hungarian-born citizens showed no interest in living as neighbours to one another. Even though there seemed a disproportionate number of them on the top block of Albany, there never existed a Hungarian quarter in any part of Toronto, and when new immigrants arrived from Hungary, they spread themselves across the city. The first small wave of Hungarians to hit Toronto arrived in the late 1920s and were mainly of rural origins and cash-strapped. In the immediate post-World War II years, members of the dispossessed Hungarian upper classes found their way to Toronto, and in the wake of the 1956 anti-communist uprising in Budapest, flocks of mostly young men trained as draftsmen and mechanics, skilled at work in factories, swelled the city's Hungarian population. If all of these former citizens of Hungary were unalike in background and education, they were alike in a shared aversion to ghetto residence. They didn't care to live together, but, as it turned out, they liked to shop together, and mostly by happenstance, the common shopping district evolved in a five-block section of Bloor West.

Within this small area, Hungarian merchants peddled food and merchandise in an atmosphere and language that turned Bloor into a corner of old Budapest. Debrenceni sausage at Elizabeth Meat & Delicatessen. All the makings for goulash and for turos czusza at the Pure Food Market. Ornate pastries at the Budapest Bakery. There was a Hungarian pharmacy, Gyosyszenten. And there were restaurants — the Continental, Taragota, L'Europe — where shakers of paprika stood alongside the salt and pepper and where the menus came in Hungarian both with and without English translation. Terra Sports & Gifts at 454 Bloor sold 650 copies of the Hungarian newspaper *Kanadai*

Once the original Bloor Theatre, a Famous Player's showcase, this building went through a period as a Chinese restaurant and emerged in the late 1980s as a showcase for experimental rock music.

"Reputable since 1955," reads the sign at the right of Dupont Street's Vesta Lunch. Reputable for what? Mostly for good'n'greasy fried stuff served twenty-four hours a day.

Magyarsag every Saturday, and a few doors east of Terra, the newspaper itself was planned, edited and printed on a rotary press. *Kanadai Magyarsag* prided itself on a weekly circulation of 11,000, a figure that made it the most read Hungarian-language newspaper outside of Hungary.

But by the late 1980s, Hungary was in retreat from Bloor. L'Europe closed its doors. Terra Sports & Gifts became a non-Hungarian cheese shop. *Kanadai Magyarsag* moved to the suburbs. Dr. Baranyi, unofficial mayor, not to mention notary, stamp dealer and driving instructor, grew old and died. And Budapest Bakery went through many metamorphoses before emerging under new ownership as a toy store. Of the major Hungarian stores, only Elizabeth Meat & Delicatessen survived, and the five blocks of Bloor returned to its old status as a mixed-bag street catering to a wide spectrum of contemporary tastes. Sushi restaurants. Health food stores. Outlets for the chains: Blockbuster, Taco Bell, Second Cup. The Annex's Hungarian period had passed.

THE MOST EXCLUSIVE HANGOUT in the Annex, the York Club, occupies its most beautiful building, the house built at the northeast corner of Bloor and St. George for George Gooderham between the years 1889 and 1892. Gooderham riches came principally from booze. George's father, William, co-founded Gooderham & Worts in 1832 as a Toronto grain mill, then set it on the path to a status as the British Empire's largest distillery. William also made his mark and his money in banking, realty and railroads. This meant there was plenty of inheritance to go around, even though there were more than plenty of Gooderhams to share in the wealth; George himself had twelve siblings and eleven children. Of all the members of this abundant family, it was George who left to Toronto the most significant and lasting physical monument in the form of the mansion at 135 St. George.

The man who designed George's residence, David Roberts, was effectively the Gooderham family's in-house architect. He provided the design brains behind much of the massive collection of Gooderham & Worts buildings close to the waterfront in old Toronto's east end. For the family's financial headquarters, Roberts came up with the handsome and commanding Gooderham Building, also known as the "flatiron building" for its triangular shape, at the convergence of Wellington and Front Streets. And he kept the Gooderhams in gorgeous housing. In 1883, he produced the Victorian mansion at 592 Sherbourne, which later became the Selby Hotel, for George's brother Charles, and sixteen years later, he set up George's son, also named George, in a Richardsonian-Romanesque pile at 504 Jarvis Street.

But the St. George house was Roberts' ultimate piece of design, Richardsonian-Romanesque with a soul. Its harmonious arrangement of stone and brick, a tower, Gothic

The most popular spot on Bloor West for coffee and a bite to eat is Dooney's, home to, among others, the lefty literary crowd.

gables, chimneys and pillared porch roused both awe and fond appreciation. So did the rooms that lay beyond the front door, done in welcoming proportions and splendid in oak and walnut and tiger maple. The much respected Toronto architecture critic and teacher Eric Arthur was an ardent admirer of the house and a frequent visitor to it when it became the quarters for the York Club. As an instance of the emotion the building generated, Arthur described in his book, *No Mean City,* an occasion when he dined at the club with the influential American architect Frank Lloyd Wright. Wright spent his formative years in Chicago, home of many buildings and houses designed by architects who found inspiration directly and indirectly in H.H. Richardson. "Students had been invited to meet the great man," Arthur wrote of Wright's evening at the York Club, "and they stood entranced as [Wright] touched mouldings with his hand, and recalled as in a dream the days of his youth sixty years before in Chicago. In whatever city we met subsequently, he spoke with affection of the Club at the corner of St. George and Bloor."

In 1909, the Gooderhams sold the house to the nascent York Club, which quickly became the home away from home for well-connected Toronto gentlemen. The York Club couldn't rival the Toronto Club, established in 1835 and eventually placed in its own building at Wellington and York sixty-two years later, in age, authority or proximity to downtown offices. But it offered aesthetic pleasures in its surroundings, a superior kitchen, and a wine collection that was said to be surpassed only by the one in Osgoode Hall that serviced the elected benchers of the Law Society of Upper Canada. The membership, holding steady at about 350 for most of its first century, included from the start prominent businessmen, lawyers and distinguished representatives of the faculty at the University of Toronto. One other quality, apart from their money and their lofty status in society, marked the members until the early 1990s: all were male. By the late twentieth century, after women members were finally admitted and after the club absorbed the Toronto Ladies Club, the female contingent comprised one-third of the entire membership. This meant that a more democratic group, at least in gender terms, could appreciate from the inside the rare architecture of a unique building. "Of the few houses inspired by Richardson that are left to us," Eric Arthur wrote, "the York Club is, probably, the most striking."

⊰ EPILOGUE ⊱

MEANWHILE, AT 199 ALBANY, we discovered a tributary of Taddle Creek under our house. This happened in the late winter of 2002 when a construction crew was digging out earth from our basement to drop it three and a half feet as part of a renovation job aimed at turning the basement into an elegant suite. To the surprise of the construction guys, they found themselves sloshing around in water up to their knees. Back in 1884, the contractor A.J. Brown was paid $15,495 to contain the entire Taddle in underground pipes. Brown must have missed the branch flowing beneath the lot at 199, and that omission left the containing job in the hands of our guys. For a week, they mucked through the mini-flood, but with ingenuity and muscle, they manufactured a diversion that steered the flow of water deeper underground, away from the smart new rooms in what used to be a plain old basement.

In other news from our block of Albany, a bright young couple moved into number 203. He's a lawyer and she's an interior designer. More than one house on the block changed hands in the preceding year, one of the larger ones selling for a figure that came within a few thousand of an astronomical half million dollars. Grassroots Albany, the street environmental group, remained active, particularly with a toad project. The idea was to carry the street back to the days, more than a century ago, when Taddle Creek hadn't yet been forced underground (by contractors such as Brown and, latterly, by residents like us), and when amphibians inhabited the Taddle's banks. To that end, the Grassroots leaders distributed toad eggs to neighbours who already had ponds in their backyards or who were keen to create new ponds. In future years, with luck and good management, live toads would be croaking their tunes and munching on Albany slugs.

In a less happy vein, early in the dark of Sunday morning on the first weekend in April, vandals trashed seven or eight cars on the street. They threw bricks through the car windows, and one of the victims was our gallant 1979 Mercedes, which suffered a smashed window on the driver's side. The unapprehended and unknown vandals, we figured, couldn't have been Annex people. Annex people throw parties. When provoked, they might hurl insults. But Annex people never throw bricks.

Help us Bring Back the Toads!

This spring Grassroots Albany and their Howland friends will bring toad eggs to a pond near you. It's the start of a multi-year project to enrich our neighbourhood with amphibians. We are using toads as a pilot project because they have very simple needs and if all goes well, we may subsequently work on reintroducing frogs and other amphibians.

Over the past few years we've all been working on restoring the local forest: planting trees, shrubs and plants that once grew here on the banks of Taddle Creek. As a result we're seeing many more butterflies, birds, dragonflies, and other forms of life.

But not everything can fly here: amphibians can't easily find their way to us across major roads. We're going to give them a lift.

Why?

Everywhere, amphibians are losing their living space. Wetlands are the most threatened of all wild habitats. We can't replace a natural wetland, but we have an extraordinary opportunity: our large lots, spring floods, and restoration efforts provide habitat unmatched elsewhere in the city.

This area was once a wetland. If we're lucky toads will patrol our gardens, munching slugs and insects, singing their springtime songs as they did long before we were here. Our children will get to know nature in their own neighbourhood, and we'll be part of a richer, healthier ecosystem.

When?

American Toads breed in early spring; anytime from late March to early May, depending on the weather. We'll probably have just a couple of days notice: as soon as breeding happens we need to collect eggs for our ponds. That's why we need to hear from you now. We'll make arrangements with you to deliver the eggs, and when the time comes, we hope to be able to give you a couple of day's notice.

We'd like to hear from you if:

- you have a pond and would like to stock it with toad eggs
- your children are interested in getting involved (kids: feel free to call Eric and Daniel, number below)
- you have seasonal flooding: it may be one of the lost tributaries of Taddle Creek!
- you want to find out how to make an amphibian-friendly pond
- you have seen or heard amphibians in the neighbourhood, even if it was a long time ago
- you want to know more about amphibians or how to help them thrive in our local forest

Who we are:

Grassroots Albany has been working with their neighbours on local environmental projects for more than a decade. Now we're joined by Ross MacCulloch, Assistant curator at the Royal Ontario Museum and other eager Howlanders with a longing for amphibians.

Call or email

Mel Greif: 531-8628, mdgreif13@hotmail.com
Faye Sims: 944-3440; tim.brook@utoronto.ca
Amanda McConnell: 537-3739; a.m@attcanada.net
kid's coordinators, Eric and Daniel: 531-5547

....see over for The Frog-Friendly Backyard

❧ BIBLIOGRAPHY ❧

Arthur, Eric. *No Mean City.* Toronto: University of Toronto Press, 1961.

Baldwin, R.M. & J. *The Baldwin and the Great Experiment.* Don Mills, Longmans, 1969.

Boire, Gary. *Morley Callaghan: The Literary Anarchist.* Toronto: ECW Press, undated.

Buchanan, Marshall. "Inventory and Natural History of the Albany Neighbourhood Forest." 1995. A report for members of Grassroots Albany.

Burton, Lydia and David Morley, eds. "The Annex Book," unpublished manuscript, 1978. Available at the Metropolitan Toronto Reference Library.

Callaghan, Barry. *Barrelhouse Kings.* Toronto: Little Brown, 1997

Careless, J.M.S. *Toronto to 1918.* Toronto: James Lorimer & Co., 1984.

Chadwick, E.M. *Monograph of the Cathedral of St. Alban the Martyr Toronto.* Published by the Cathedral, 1920.

Cohen, Matt. *Typing.* Toronto: Random House, 2000.

Eaton, Flora McCrae. *Memory's Wall: The Autobiography of Flora McCrae Eaton.* Toronto: Clarke Irwin, 1956

Fetherling, Douglas. *Travels By Night.* Toronto: Lester Publishing, 1994.

Fetherling, Douglas. *Way Down Deep in the Belly of the Beast.* Toronto: Lester Publishing, 1997.

Filey, Michael. *A Toronto Album.* Toronto: University of Toronto Press, 1970.

Gatenby, Greg. Toronto: *A Literary Guide.* Toronto: McArthur & Company, 1999.

Jones, Frank. *The Master and the Maid.* Toronto: Irwin, 1985.

Kilbourn, William. *Toronto Remembered: A Celebration of the City.* Toronto: Stoddart, 1984.

Lee, Dennis. *Nightwood: New and Selected Poems 1965-1996*. Toronto: M&S, 1996.

Lemon, James. *Toronto Since 1918*. Toronto: James Lorimer & Co., 1985.

Lemon, James. "The Annex: A Brief Historical Geography to 1986." The Annex Residents' Association, undated. City of Toronto Archives.

Litvack, Marilyn M. *Edward James Lennox: Master Builder*. Toronto: Dundurn Press, 1995.

Lundell, Liz. *The Estates of Old Toronto*. Erin: Boston Mills Press, 1997.

Martyn, Lucy Booth. *Aristocratic Toronto: Nineteenth Century Grandeur*. Toronto: Gage, 1980.

McHugh, Patricia. *Toronto Architecture: A City Guide*. Toronto: M&S, 1989.

McQueen, Rod. *The Eatons*. Toronto: Stoddart, 1998.

Nowlan, David and Nadine. *The Bad Trip*. Toronto: House of Anansi, 1970.

Scadding, Henry. *Toronto of Old*. 1873. Reprint. Toronto: Oxford University Press, 1966.

Scott, Kenneth. *Dealing With Dragons*. Published by St. George's College, Toronto, 1984.

Sebert, John. *The Nabes: Toronto's Wonderful Neighbourhood Movie Houses*. Oakville: Mosaic Press, 2001.

Sullivan, Rosemary. *The Shadow Maker: The Life of Gwendolyn MacEwen*. Toronto: HarperCollins, 1995.

Sullivan, Rosemary. *Red Shoes: Margaret Atwood Starting Out*. Toronto: HarperCollins, 1998.

⇥ ACKNOWLEDGMENTS ⇤

The following people and institutions were invaluable in providing information and photographs for this book: the Metropolitan Toronto Reference Library, the Palmerston branch of the Metropolitan Toronto Library, the Toronto Archives, the Ontario Archives, the Osgoode Hall Library, Maria Halonen, the Finnish Weekly Newspaper, Temma Gentles, Robert Fulford, Diane Gee, Philippa Campsie, John Kerr and Father David Donkin of Royal St. George's College, Don Borthwick and Margie Halling of the University of Toronto Schools Alumni Association, Karen Teeple, Alec Scott, Elizabeth Wilson and Ian Montagnes.

⇥ PHOTO CREDITS ⇤

INDEX